Two Acre Eden

Two Acre Eden

Gene Logsdon

 Rodale Press   Emmaus, PA

Book design by Nora Bullock

Printed in the United States of America on recycled
paper, containing a high percentage of de-inked fiber.

Library of Congress Cataloging in Publication Data

Logsdon, Gene.
  Two acre Eden.

  Includes bibliographical references and index.
  1. Organic gardening. 2. Gardening. I. Title.
SB453.5.L63 1980   635'.04'8   79-23920
ISBN 0-87857-290-2 hardcover
ISBN 0-87857-308-9 paperback

2 4 6 8 10 9 7 5 3 1 hardcover
2 4 6 8 10 9 7 5 3 1 paperback

Contents

Contents

Introduction
to the Revised Edition

The first edition of this book was written ten years ago. Since then our family has moved from our original Two Acre Eden in Pennsylvania to a 32-acre Eden in Ohio. It seems easier to tell you that in the Introduction than to go through the whole book and qualify the verbs in every chapter to reflect that change accurately.

The change was essentially a move "back home." From my pasture hill I can now see the silos of the farm where I grew up and worked as a younger man, and that explains the move, too. Since the popular wisdom says, "You can't go home again," I had to prove, with typical bullheadedness, that you could go home again. Also it seemed at the time, that if 2 acres could prove to be Eden-like, then 32 acres ought to be 15 times more enjoyable. I think the most helpful hint I could give you in this book is to say that ain't necessarily so. Living on a larger acreage out in the country may suit bullheaded and contrary independents like myself, but I'm convinced that saner people can enjoy 2 acres more than they can enjoy 32 or even 22. When you grow food intensively for fun and for practicality while holding down another job, which is what most of us have to do, even 2 acres can become a mighty big chunk of earth. I'm also convinced that 2 acres in the hands of a skilled gardener will produce more food and enjoyment than 32 in the hands of a harried homesteader who likes to partake of off-farm hobbies and vacations in addition to a heavy off-farm job. What my wife and I do now is too much work for most gardeners, but a Two Acre Eden such as we managed for ten years is easily within the grasp of anyone who enjoys homelife, the camaraderie of a real neighborhood, and the satisfaction of providing at least part of his or her own necessities of life.

In the interest of updating the progress of homestead technology, I have added new information. For example, if ten years ago someone had told me that I would heat my home in 1978 almost entirely with a wood stove, I would have urged that person to talk to a psychiatrist. But heating our home with wood is exactly what we are doing — and is what thousands of homeowners are doing — and so I have added the fruits of what I've learned after quite an involved experience with wood heating.

I also revised some of my irreverent remarks about organic gardening (though not many I made about chemical gardening), because in ten years my knowledge of and appreciation for ecological gardening methods have deepened considerably. However, whenever I've figured I could get away with it, I've tried to continue to poke a little fun at both sides of the organic-chemical controversy, not because the subject is not a serious one, but because those of us closely involved in it tend to take ourselves too seriously sometimes.

In general, I think the book still does what I wanted it to do ten years ago, that is, provide first of all a sympathetic shoulder for gardeners to lean on and grin a little. Scores of letters from readers of the first edition attest to that need, and so I have added a substantial number of chapters that might seem to be — and are — entirely humorous in nature. However, truth is often served better by humor than by sober-sided instruction, and I hope that if you find a smile here and there you will also find right beside it a hint or two of practical wisdom that help your homesteading and backyard ventures at least as much as the keenest and most detailed instructional information you might find elsewhere. I could write a very long chapter on how to take care of a riding horse, but if instead, I can dissuade you from the madness of keeping one on a small lot, I will have done you a greater service — even if your teenage daughter hates me forever.

The idea of a Two Acre Eden is, in fact, more pertinent today than it was ten years ago. With rumors of fuel shortages in the wind and the certainty that prices will be very high in the future for all kinds of fossil resources, we will have to make significant changes in our life-styles. We are going to learn again the simpler joys of home living— and that is what this book is all about.

Chapter 1

Home Is
Where Your Heart Is
and Vice Versa
Even More So

For Sale: Farmhouse in good condition and two acres. Gently rolling, good springs, stream, and well. Orchard. Small village and good school three miles. Population density controlled and land forever zoned by immutable law from airports, highways, apartments, and factories. $30,000. More land if desired.

Almost all the gardeners I've crossed hoes with in the last 30 years are combing the classified sections of newspapers every Sunday looking for that ad. Including me. Of course we aren't going to find it, and we know that. But deep inside is a dream, an inner madness, that a place does exist on this tired old earth where pollution is only a word in the dictionary and a man could mark time by the fall of flower petals. There is joy in the seeking.

Gardening is my weakness, or one of them anyway. Puttering in the soil is considered a harmless avocation, but I know it is also a symptom of certain deep-rooted if not dangerous irregularities. For example, I love serenity and order, an abnormality in modern times that I manage to disguise by keeping my desk in a constant state of havoc and disarray. Any noise over 50 decibels, whether it's the Beatles or Beethoven, makes me apoplectic. Seeing beer cans thrown out of car windows propels me into a rage, and I consider crowds a dread. I prefer people in small, intimate doses. And I hide among my cornstalks. Maybe there I will discover, as Mendel did with his peas, something ten times more valuable to man than all the conventions, assemblies, congregations, demonstrations, committees, and convocations in history.

I am also a frustrated artist, which is why I hoe weeds with such mad compulsion. The hoe is my brush, the garden my canvas. I want to make pictures by arranging nature according to my own design. Much of the time I just stand in front of the vegetable rows, admiring my weedless handiwork.

Like every genuine gardener, I am insanely land-hungry and would much rather own an acre of meadow than a Cadillac or a yacht. I drool over those alluring notices of five-dollars-an-acre land in Brazil I will never see, read homesteading information I will never use, and retire mentally to an island or mountain fortress I will share only with other humanists as brilliant as I. Leading every back-to-the-land movement is the frustrated gardener. He socks his spade into the earth and hopes to strike paradise.

There must be more frustrated gardeners than I suspected, because the back-to-the-country rash is breaking out again—as it does about every 20 years. I know young family men who are actually giving up high salaries to escape the cities for what they think is a more human environment in the country. Others, like me, who work in cities but are natives of rural areas and ought to know better, are getting the bug and hauling out all those old books (and many new ones) on subsistence farming. Most of the books were written by people who never really tried to live off the land but went back to the farm carrying a typewriter. You can go into the ghettos any day and find a recent refugee from subsistence farming who decided correctly that anything was better than that.

I said as much to a young back-to-the-lander I met in town the other day. He had one of Euell Gibbons' books on living on wild food in one hand and in the other, a mimeographed list of government lands for sale, rolled up, which he used as a sort of gavel to emphasize his points of view. "Oh, that may be true," he replied. "But we've got something your typewriter players and your poverty-stricken refugees don't have. We've got know-how. We're going to profit by former homesteading mistakes. And we're going to use technology—after all, technology's been using us. We don't intend to be purists about this."

That reminded me of the family I'd met that built a swimming pool on their mini-farm ten miles from Lake Erie's beaches. I asked them why. "Well, for one thing I can afford the pool now," said the head of the house with a smile. (That's technology.) "Lake Erie is so polluted we hardly dare swim in it anyway." (That's technology.) "Besides, even going ten miles to the lake gets us in an awful traffic jam, not to mention the human jam on the beach—it's so covered with bodies you can't find the sand." (That's probably technology's fault too.) "And look. I sit here by the pool, watch a ball game on TV, which is followed by a tour through the Winterthur Museum, which is followed by an interview with the vice-president. Traveling is a dangerous and exhausting expedient I can avoid. Everything comes to me. Soon we'll have videophones and we can visit distant friends without leaving the living room. Electronics gets rid of the one weakness of my earthly paradise. No more boredom."

Most people starting new homes in the country or outer suburbs now give ecology as their reason for moving. Or the lack of it. "Whether our move was practical or not didn't really matter," one young mother said. "Pollution, not only waste, but the pollution of the whole human system was getting to be more than we could endure, physically or mentally. We didn't really feel we had a choice."

"That's only half a reason," her husband added

3

quickly. "Actually, ecology conveys the idea that an earthly paradise might be possible after all. Younger people empathize with that. They don't all believe in nonearthly paradises anymore. If heaven is going to be, it had better be now."

None of these reasons for moving to the country was quite adequate to explain the yearnings that led me to establish my Two Acre Eden. I was not as upset as I probably should have been about pollution, nor did I feel that the Establishment was suppressing my individuality. My motivation seemed to spring from a need for that special, essential identity and satisfaction that come from a sense of home, a sense of place. Having left the land of my roots, as so many of us have had to do, I missed the well-being I used to feel by living in one spot a long time and knowing that this was my place.

I wanted to walk along a creek with my son and be able to tell him that when I was a boy I slipped into the water at the same spot where he fell in. I wanted to plow the soil my father and grandfather had plowed. Or sit under a tree my mother planted. Or at least to start a tree whose shade my children would enjoy. I wanted stability. Belonging. I was losing patriotism because I had no place left that I was willing to fight and die for.

I missed strolling down the street that had been laid out by my kinfolks and their neighbors 150 years ago and saying hello to all the people walking past and calling them by name because I knew them so well I knew what they dreamed about. Just as they knew me. I was losing my sense of honesty because I never stayed long enough in one place for people to find out whether I was really worth anything.

I wanted to live without hurrying so fast or running so far because there would be no place I needed to get away from or any I wanted to get to quickly. I would have my place. I was losing the power to think because I had no refuge where I could slow down long enough to comprehend reality.

About half this country is looking right now for home

—walking down alien streets, rolling down highways that lead to nowhere, jetting through the empty spaces between non-places, hungering for home.

> I think the thing we're talking about is no more or less hard to understand than the simple desire to have a home. A home, and a sense of home that can only grow out of a sense of place. Cities aren't places anymore. They're scenes projected on screens, then bulldozed away, neighborhood by neighborhood, like cancelled TV shows. People who are tired of scenes are leaving, or wanting to anyway, longing for a place, torn between the joy of getting out of town and a vague despair that maybe there ain't no such thing as place after all, that maybe all there is to do is ride around in outfitted buses, floating along the bloodless traffic arteries of the world.*

I've developed my Two Acre Eden to about half its potential. Already it has given me, my wife Carol, my children Jenny and Jerry, a sense of permanence, of identity. It has been the scene of some of our most precious family moments; it has been a place of high adventure, of great emotional sharing; it has provided a setting for peeling off layers down to our most creative selves; it has been a place of love and a place of peace.

However, you can't talk favorably about anything in the United States unless you can show that it will make a profit. Unfortunately, this is the standard by which all things under our particular sun must be measured and the chief reason our quality of living has been going downhill.

You *can* make your garden pay. You can make a good living on a five-acre vegetable or plant nursery farm and some people do. But if you accomplish this, your

*From the best-selling *Whole Earth Catalog* (which may well be in its peculiarly winsome way the most significant publication printed in the years 1969/70), March 1970, p. 28 in the editor's introduction to Wendell Berry's excerpt from his essay *A Native Hill.*

modern homestead will no longer be a refuge for your spirit, but part and parcel of the backbreaking, mind-straining world of competitive business. In fact, to make a good living on a small farm is one of the most difficult businesses around. It takes a cross between a genius and a slave, and very few people are up to it.

So read all those books that have come out periodically over the last 100 years on how to gain independence on five acres with a spoonful of salt or two. These books are good for dreaming and contain very useful information, but the blissful independence they conjure up between the lines is fake.

By and by I will tell you ways to make a little extra money every month of the year, since, if you are like me, that may be the only way you can afford a place in the country. But unless you are very rich, your little paradise will only be a refuge if you have an outside job, preferably one close to home. Later on, you may be able to taper it off to part-time. Or more practically perhaps, if we go to a four-day week, or even less, as some economists are predicting, you'll be right in the groove to balance a host of avocations at home against a paycheck from your outside job. You will have no trouble, believe me, with what prophets are fancifully calling the New Problem of Leisure. You will not be condemned to spending all that mythical leisure trying to find a spot of sand between the bodies at the beach, nor waiting in mile-long queues in front of the theater, nor stuck in countless traffic jams, nor suckered into tourist attractions that claim to show you how differently other people live than you do. Or even getting plastered on a case of beer in the backyard for lack of something better to do.

Being a loyal, red-blooded American, I still find it necessary to beard the financial lions and assert that many of the humble practices of Two Acre Eden are profitable financially. For instance, experts will tell you that you don't save any money growing your own food. "By the time you add up all your expenses on sprays, fertilizer, equipment, and your time," says a dear friend of mine, "you'll find you could have bought a whole peck of apples at the store for every one you eat off your tree."

Tain't so.

Our grocer is convinced that my wife is either nuts or the biggest put-on in the history of the consumer. Since we raise a substantial portion of the food we eat, she goes to the supermarket mostly to gloat. "Buy *that* chicken," she'll shudder quite visibly at the meat counter. "No, thank you. We raise our own." But then the very next day, as we are eating fresh strawberries from our garden, she will bounce up from the table and call the grocer. She has a note pad full of figures in front of her. "How much are strawberries today?" she wants to know.

"Is this Mrs. Logsdon?" asks a voice, in undisguised bad humor.

"Yesssss."

Long pause. Sigh of resignation.

"Well, we have a few local berries in, good ones—" he clears his voice, and adds apologetically, "—but they are pretty high. One dollar and nineteen cents a quart." Then before he can say that he has some California berries a little cheaper, she harps:

"Is that all? Why, you can't make any money that way. Are you sure you can't up that price a little more? I mean, after all, good berries are a rare commodity."

The grocer is just not used to hearing a housewife talk this way—especially one who has told him just yesterday that his meat and produce are only one step removed from garbage. He can't find anything to say. He can just wait silently until she excuses herself and hangs up. A madwoman in every community; that is the grocer's cross to bear.

But my wife is not really mad. After she puts the phone down she scratches away with a pencil on her Financial Statement. Two times $1.19 equals $2.38. She adds that to another list of figures, then informs the rest of the family, "So far, we've eaten $66.64 worth of strawberries."

I counter: "But we could have driven over to the strawberry farm and gotten them for 90¢ a quart."

Two Acre Eden

"*Consumer Reports* says you have to figure car costs at 17¢ a mile," she reminds me. "But even if you use the 90¢ figure, we have still eaten $50.40 worth, and there's another 50 quarts out in the garden."

The point is, raising your own food does pay, mostly because what you eat you would have purchased retail. And any farmer who could figure his production gross at retail prices without the costs of retail marketing would be a very successful farmer indeed.

We did get 100 quarts of strawberries from our little patch that year. Most we ate or froze and some we sold. We figured our gross to be about $60, and that's conservative because it would be almost impossible to buy berries of as good a quality as these. Our expenses? Twelve dollars for plants (I could have used first-year runners from the old patch if I had really wanted to scrimp) and about 50¢ worth of fertilizer. If you want to get technical, I suppose there was a penny's worth of wear and tear on my spade and garden rake. Technically also, I ought to figure in the taxes on that plot of ground, though I'd have to pay those anyway.

"But your time," my economic expert reminds me. "You have to figure that in too."

Indeed I do. I estimate over a year I devote about ten hours to strawberries. Hours that could have been spent playing golf at a dollar a hole, more or less depending upon what happened at the 19th hole. Or driving at 17¢ a mile to some noted attraction somewhere, $3 a head. Or opening my stomach to the danger of ulcers by worrying about the office work I should have gotten finished on Friday when I was worrying about the work I should have finished on Thursday. In other words, the more I figure in my "time," the more profitable my strawberries become Not to mention that I happen to enjoy growing strawberries.

"Maybe you have a good record for strawberries, which are comparatively expensive, but what about something like apples," my friend continues, undeterred. "You can buy a whole bushel of apples for under five bucks, and that won't even cover the cost of spraying your tree every year." He thinks he has me there, only he's made a grave mistake because now he is going to have to listen to my whole diatribe on garden economics and miss the ball game on TV.

"Listen, you blighted offcast of computer economics," I growl. "You know I'm the most parsimonious soul this side of Vermont. Look at my sprayer. It cost $12. I've used it to spray three apple trees, six peach trees, three pear trees, and five cherry trees for five years, and I think it will last five more. I put on two dormant oil sprays in the spring. This can of Volck dormant oil spray costs $9.98, but there is enough in it to spray one apple tree every spring for ten years. And these days, that's all the spraying I do. I used to spray my trees every weekend with a mixture of captan for fungal diseases and Malathion for bugs. But I've found out that I don't really need to do it unless we get some kind of plague. The only difference is that some of my fruit is wormy and some of it gets scab or brown rot. Now a commercial orchardist can't afford poor fruit because he can't sell it. For home use, it doesn't really matter. What I lose is less in value than what the spray would cost. And even without spraying, a good percentage of the crop keeps ripening just as pretty as a picture anyhow."

"All right, all right, I give up," says my friend. But now that I am on the soapbox, I do not intend to relent so quickly.

"The crucial factor in garden economics is how much you use of what you raise. I know people who spend ten bucks spraying an apple tree and then let the apples rot because the housewife won't *use* them. She'd rather spend that time parading in front of the supermarket against higher food prices. We eat apples fresh, pied, sauced, and juiced. The nicest ones may go as gifts to friends instead of some worthless five-dollar trinket. The chickens get the really wormy ones. And furthermore, I can't always buy the varieties of apples I like best. I wouldn't trade a tree-ripened Macoun or a Stayman Winesap from a tree on a north slope for a whole bushel of Red Delicious." I am fairly ranting now.

"You know, you can easily overequip yourself on a small homestead. Some people buy a $2,000 garden tractor to mow a lawn that requires no more than a $200 machine. Or they purchase a $600 rotary tiller for a small garden they could easily turn over with a spade. That's why gardening doesn't seem to pay."

"Quit shouting," says my friend. And then he thinks of one more objection.

"Well, you simply wouldn't eat that many strawberries if you had to buy them."

True. And that's the biggest payoff of all.

Chapter 2

Of Course I'm an Organic Gardener; I Just Keep That Sprayer Around for the Neighbors to Borrow

I did not come to organic gardening easily. I was backing away from the danger I perceived in chemical farming, when I tripped over the organic threshold and fell through the rear door. It is very difficult to explain this to an urban organic gardener who has never tilled more than 50 square feet in any one year. In the Cornbelt we were raised up fervently believing that not using commercial fertilizers was nearly as bad as not going to church on Sunday. If I were to go into New York City and advocate the abolishment of taxi service, the response would be no different than what commercial farmers think when a gardener journeys to the countryside and advocates the abolishment of anhydrous ammonia. Old farm acquaintances of mine still think there is something pinko-commie about biological farming and say that I have betrayed them when I say nasty things about herbicides.

On the other hand, when I tell fervent organicists that I used to work as hard for *Farm Journal* as I now do for *Organic Gardening,* they assume that some sort of dramatic conversion must have taken place. Perhaps I was

11

born again, like President Carter? Perhaps a thunderbolt knocked me from a horse, as happened to Saint Paul, while I was riding to deliver a diatribe against organic gardening methods? Perhaps I had a vision of J. I. Rodale seated at the right hand of God?

I've been knocked off more than one horse, but the only things I ever saw when I looked up were hooves coming at me. I try to garden organically because it seems a practical and interesting way to raise good food. I seek neither cult nor religion. If there is a philosophy consciously or unconsciously propelling me toward organic horticulture, it is my conviction that a healthy democracy or republic rests on self-reliant and independent citizens. If organic living promotes self-reliance, I'm for it. It is only lately that I begin to see glimmerings of a deeper meaning to it all; that the principles of ecology bind all things together. If we do not learn an ecological method of producing food that preserves the whole food chain, then it will not preserve the evolutionary wonder called man either. Ignoring ecology in food production and other human activities, we are ignoring humanness and destroying ourselves. But these are only glimmerings, and I do not yet see the conclusions. For now I do what I do on my homestead because it makes me happy. I write about it in hope that it will help others to be happy too.

My family, like others whose roots run deep in farming tradition, is fond of an old refrain that farmers of long ago used to repeat as they planted corn, four seeds to a hill:

> One for the cutworm,
> One for the crow,
> One for the gopher,
> And one to grow.

Modern agriculture has rendered that refrain obsolete. Today a farmer can plant 25,000 kernels of corn per acre (yes, he knows precisely how many kernels he's planting) and be reasonably sure that 24,900 of them will grow to maturity. The technological advances in machinery, chemicals, and improved seed that make accomplishments like this possible, are of course fantastic, and not the least result is that the specter of famine becomes more remote every day—or so it has seemed.

But solving one problem seems to have created others. It is questionable whether the farmer himself is any better off. If we were to update that old bit of verse, it would have to go like this:

> One for the banker,
> One for the tax fee,
> One for the overhead,
> And one for me.

In replacing one set of hazards with another, the farmer finds that he can make ends meet only by producing more per man-hour than he did before. The most effective way to produce more per man-hour is to farm more land, which drives half the neighbors out of business, thereby providing cities with more people than they can handle. Then America sits back pompously bragging to the world how one of our wonderfully efficient farmers can produce enough food for 58 people. Leaving the 58 presumably free to follow worthwhile pursuits, like, for instance, blowing up colleges, fighting someone else's wars, and running for public offices that nobody needs. Then to top off the whole frosty business, we find that millions of our own Americans suffer from malnutrition: some don't get enough food, some don't get the right food, and even the well-fed majority is eating an alarming quantity of additives, preservatives, and other chemicals that may be harmful.

A great many thoughtful people are now wondering if all the problems of our times aren't somehow linked together in some fuzzy sort of way, oversimplistically stated by an old farmer I know: "We've worked up quite a lather. There ain't enough honest jobs left to go around."

Thoughtful people first try to do something about problems at the public level and often find, to their dismay, no one who can make a decision. As Karl Bednarik says in his book *The Male in Crisis* (New York: Knopf, 1970), "Conditions in our world are such that an ever diminishing number of men can make all the vital decisions for an ever increasing number of people."

Thoughtful people, becoming frustrated, decide to ameliorate conditions in modern living that for them are becoming unendurable, on a personal level. They begin by establishing their own little worlds, practical Two Acre Edens, where they can exercise a certain amount of choice over the way they live. It is not a form of copping out. If enough people follow them, we could fire all those expensive presidential commissions on city and rural problems and put half our politicians to honest work like raising squash.

But a Two Acre Eden provides more than a home-grown food supply, and the word gardening becomes something less than adequate. A research report entitled: "Where It Is Still Pleasant to Live in the USA" uses a better term, "The Garden Way of Living" defined as: "essentially productive living on an acre or more of land, in the open country perhaps, but more likely in or near a town or small city. It is a distinctive way of life—distinct from professional farming, distinct from metropolitan living, distinct from living in the crowded expensive suburbs on the peripheries of the great cities. It is for all age groups—the young and ambitious as well as the elderly and retired."

Another term, or perhaps I should say, philosophy, that describes to some degree the thinking behind the life system of a typical Two Acre Eden is Organic Living. The concept of Organic Living started with organic gardeners, who believe in gardening without inorganic fertilizers and poison sprays. Such gardeners used to be considered a queer bunch, sort of a religious cult, but now that ecology is all the rage, they are becoming modern-day heroes. Most of what ecologists are proclaiming, organic gardeners have been saying since the 1940s, when J. I. Rodale started *Organic Farming and Gardening* magazine.

The ideas behind Organic Living go far beyond pro-

14

hibitions against man-made chemicals. Broadly speaking, organicists say that man must learn to live in harmony with nature, must take his proper place in the biologic food chain, must learn to live the only way he can continue to live healthfully — preserving his environment and tuning in to the rhythms of nature. Ecologists can say it with more flourish, but that's about the gist of it.

What I admire about organic gardeners is that they don't just talk about ecology and cleaning up pollution. They, as individuals, practice it in their own homes and gardens. They realize that by the time the government gets around to improving the environment, we may all be dead.

I guess that makes me an organicist. Trouble is, I've been known to be a backslider. I know that composting and mulching are the best techniques for soil improvement, but when no one is looking, I have succumbed to temptation and slipped a little 10-10-10 fertilizer under the mulch. Or at least I used to before learning what a waste of money that was. When the larvae of pine sawflies begin to gobble my evergreens, my passions flare up, and I descend upon them with a vengeance and a sprayer full of Malathion, even though in the long run I've learned this only prolongs the problem.

Although there are a few farms where organic methods are used exclusively, I don't expect every commercial farmer to suddenly start mulching and composting 3,000 acres of crops. But the small gardener or the owner of a Two Acre Eden, where commercial production is not a necessity for financial stability, can get along without help from the chemical industry. I say that with some reservations. I've gardened successfully without chemicals and inorganic fertilizers, and I've had failures that way too. The subject is complex in the extreme. I find myself trying to devise a way to lay the whole pro-and-con argument out on paper in just a few sentences, so that all may grasp, in a trice, the whole truth. It's impossible. No one knows the whole truth.

If you decide to abjure chemicals and other pollution-causing materials, be prepared to endure certain uncom-

fortable consequences. Earth is not the loving Mother the
ecologically minded sometimes make her out to be. If all
the poison ivy in the world would disappear tomorrow, I
defy any ecologist to find any harm done to the environment. But if you decide poison ivy is better than herbicides,
then be ready to doctor your children when they come
home with a rash of it. Or pull the stuff out by hand,
and get a good dose yourself. I have.

A biochemist I know, whose avocation is gardening,
switched to pure organic methods a couple of years ago.
(When a biochemist gets that concerned, I listen to what
he has to say.) While he says he has been able to control
bugs without chemicals, he admits that he has found no
organic method to stop fungal diseases. "When my roses
develop black spot severely, I just let them die."

I followed this fatalistic philosophy with my peach
trees this year. During a wetter than usual spring and
early summer, I watched brown rot completely destroy my
crop—except for one tree. Again complexity. Why didn't
this tree of peaches rot? It was an earlier variety
than the others (the trees were planted before I bought
the place; to my knowledge this peach is Early Elberta,
but I'm not positively certain), which would seem to mean
that brown rot is most vicious at some particular point
in the fruit's development or that this particular variety
is more resistant. Also interesting, I think, is the fact that
I have not been able to find an expert willing to help
me solve this riddle. I get a shrug and a word of advice:
"You should have sprayed."

I suspect that most spraying in small gardens is
simply a way to cover a tankful of ignorance. I notice that
the USDA's experiemental farm at Beltsville, Maryland,
agrees that a good way to control slugs is to put shallow
saucers of beer in the garden. Organic gardeners have
been doing that for years. The slugs love the beer, fall into
the saucers, and drown.

There are many effective, nonpoisonous bug control
practices. A drop of mineral oil on the newly emerging
silk of each ear of sweet corn will keep out worms about

as well as DDT. A New Jersey grower harvests a large crop of summer squash (30 acres), without pesticides. He mulches the plants with aluminum foil, which, for reasons no one is quite sure of, scares away aphids and squash bugs. The old-fashioned control for squash bugs was to lay shingles or boards beside the squash plants. The bugs would crawl under the shingles at night, and early in the morning, the gardener simply lifted the shingles and stomped the bugs.

Organic gardeners always have believed that marigold roots somehow drive away soil nematodes, and just recently science has found supporting evidence that this is true. Some growers claim that marigolds planted between bean rows will keep bean beetles away, a practice that in my experience is proved about 60 percent effective.

I've watched gardeners lose their heads over an outbreak of tomato worms or potato bugs and inundate their plants with spray when it wasn't necessary. If they'd have just kept their cool and brushed half a dozen of the tomato worms off into a jar, their troubles would have been over. The first year that I decided I would NOT spray or dust my potatoes, I hand-picked 37 potato bug larvae (actual count) from my 100-foot row, a few at a time as they appeared. I suppose I spent a whole 15 minutes at this task. I got the nicest potato crop I ever grew.

Japanese beetles attacked our roses and grape leaves with a real vengeance that year too. We almost panicked. But instead of spraying, all four members of the family started to collect Japanese beetles. We found that in the evening, the beautifully iridescent green bugs wouldn't fly away readily, and each of us brushed them into jars as fast as we could. After three evenings in a row, we had about four pints of beetles. End of the plague. There were still plenty of them around, and they still gobbled a few rose blossoms, but it was apparent that the tide had turned in our favor. Another nontoxic Japanese beetle control is milky spore disease, which you can buy under the trade name Doom from Fairfax Biological Laboratory, Inc., Electronic Road, Clinton Corners, NY 12514.

Too many people still think that the difference

between organic gardeners and conventional gardeners is that the former don't use chemicals. Organic growers use all kinds of chemicals, and their methods of using them are so modern they are only now coming to the attention of commercial farmers. Nova Scotian researchers for ten years controlled the codling moth in their commercial orchards quite successfully, in some cases using only a biological control program and an organically approved insecticide, ryania. Ryania is an old botanical quite safe for warm-blooded animals but it gives certain insects very bad stomachaches. Rotenone and pyrethrum are two more botanicals organic growers rely on. Chemical companies are now making synthetic pyrethrums for cotton pests that have become immune to the dangerously toxic organo-phosphate compounds.

Bacillus thuringiensis, sold under the trade names of Dipel, Thuricide, and Biotrol, is fairly effective against many pest worms, particularly cabbage looper. Long used by organicists, it is now making its way into commercial agriculture. BT is safe to man and animal but paralyzes the worm's gut. The federal Environmental Protection Agency (EPA) is going through all sorts of pious preten-sions of being as strict with BT as with toxic chemicals, and won't clear it for everything just yet. I use it on my grapes and fruit trees whether approved or not, since I'm not selling these fruits.

Miscible oil is a safe insecticide for dormant fruit trees, long used by both organic and chemical fruit growers. Lately, a new use has been found for it. In the West, the pest, pear psylla has become immune to many of the hard, toxic chemicals. Biological control scientists learned that a simple spray of cold water with a little oil and a synthetic pyrethrum in it at precisely the right time will kill the egg-laying females and so control the pest at a fraction of the cost of former sprays, which didn't work.

When tent caterpillars spin their webs in fruit trees in the spring, they can ruin a branch in a couple of days. Should you rush for the sprayer? Instead, wait till evening when all the worms crawl back inside their nest. Get a pole that will reach the web, tie a small, kerosene-soaked rag around one end, light it, and burn the web out. A recent gardening book makes fun of this practice as tedious, old-fashioned, and dangerous. I disagree. I can burn out a dozen webs while you're getting your sprayer ready. And that little flame on the end of the pole isn't half as dangerous as breathing in the spray that comes drifting back down out of the tree into your eyes, nose, and mouth.

Corn borers can be controlled by hand-picking very effectively and with very little effort (I found to my surprise) in a *small* patch. Right after the corn tassels come out, go down the rows observing closely the main stem of the tassel. When you see small mounds of sawdustlike particles, it means there is a borer inside. Just pry open the tassel stem with your fingernails and when you see the borer, squeeze the stalk together, smashing the little varmint.

Lots of people are too squeamish for such work. In fact, one of the less noble traits of our sophisticated society is a fervid horror of bugs and worms. Yet half the population of the world supplements its diet with bugs and worms, which are very rich in protein. When I say, as I do so love to, that worms in cherries do not hurt you (too many cherries is what gives you a stomachache) but are in fact good for you, the usual reply is: "Ugh. That's not funny."

If the housewife . . .

Would quit turning up her nose at a harmless scab on an apple;

Would realize that the tastiest garden produce does not necessarily look like the *Ladies' Home Journal Cookbook*-image of perfection photographs;

Would learn that an egg with a little chicken dirt on the shell might be fresher and more nutritious than that shiny, old, super-Grade A in the stores;

Would recognize that a corn earworm isn't half as ugly as the chemical residue building up in her mammary glands;

Would admit that the ant crawling across the floor isn't going to hurt the baby, but that the half-can of insecticide she sprays to kill it might . . .

THEN, the commercial grower can stop using half the sprays the demands of the marketplace now force him to use.

For years I had a neighbor, Fred, who did not believe in mulch, or hoes either. He did an excellent job of controlling weeds with chemicals. But something of a marvelous transformation occurred, which even he recognized. My clay became loamier each year; his, only harder. Moreover, the weed killers year after year on the same soil, began to have a carry-over effect on his vegetables. For no other apparent reason, the plants began to look spindly, while mine, close by, grew sassier. He used more inorganic fertilizer; I had to use less. My soil stayed moist during drought; his turned to concrete. When it rained, the water ran off his garden, eroding soil as it went; my mulch sopped up water like a sponge.

Having observed suburbanites over a number of years, I think they err not so much in using chemical sprays and inorganic fertilizers, but in using way too much. The city-raised suburbanite thinks a lawn is an extension of his living room rug. Somehow he has gotten the notion (aided and abetted by his friendly local garden center) that a lawn is an absolutely unblemished sward of bluegrass without a blade out of place.

Upon this grass he spends himself literally to the last drop of sweat. In spring, the lawn must be rolled. And limed. And thatched. And sprayed. And fertilized. Then mowed. And mowed. And mowed. So that every blade is exactly two inches high and not "a silly millimeter longer."

And then, the growing season over, it is the damned leaves. Every last one of them must be removed. And all this to the thunderous cacophony of his $1,200 tractor (which usually he doesn't need and can't really afford), blasting the peacefulness of every weekend. Hear, if you still can, the noble symphony of sound that ten of these perfectionists can make on a quiet Saturday afternoon. And what doth it profit them? If they persist, they may indeed have the perfect lawn eventually, which they can then sell to someone else and move to an apartment because they are too tired of "keeping up the place." They have also saturated the neighborhood with more herbicides and nitrates than could run off a 400-acre Iowa farm in two years.

They have none of the interesting weeds that could pleasure them during an occasional mowing. No dandelions to make spring's first salad; no yellow rocket to make fall's last nutritious greens. No buttercup, heal-all, daisy, violet, Queen Anne's lace to marvel at; no buck horn to cuss. And if they stop mowing and spraying long enough to gas the tractor, the crabgrass is right back again. Like the housewife who could endure only the purest white shirts no matter how many detergents and enzymes pollute the streams, he *will* have the perfect lawn. Why?

If you can't abide a sloppy lawn like mine, however, take the advice of a friend of mine who has a nice lawn and doesn't work too hard at it. "First, plant Merion bluegrass. It grows thick enough to crowd out even crabgrass. Secondly, lime your lawn well. Lime is more important than fertilizer. But I use a little fertilizer in the spring. A mixture of equal parts of soybean meal, bonemeal, and wood ashes is just as good as an application of 5-10-5 fertilizer, though more expensive. Thirdly, and most important, don't mow close or often, especially during dry weather. Set your mower so it leaves at least 2½ inches of grass, or even higher."*

When I gave up using chemical sprays on the edible products of my garden, I spent some long hours seated between the rows or under a tree, simply observing. Some of this observation was occasionally diverted by a catnap or by a book in my lap, but nonetheless, I consider my vigils quite scientific in a poetic sort of way. I had been waiting for doomsday by the hand of bugs—convinced that without insecticides it was merely a matter of time before great armies of aphids, Japanese beetles, slugs, grass-

---

*In this book, I will not give specific recommendations on how much lime and fertilizer you should use per square yard. Soil, climate, and conditions vary too much. The personnel at good garden stores will be happy to advise you.

hoppers, bean beetles, cabbageworms, earwigs, and corn earworms would reduce my garden to a desert. It never happened, but the time spent waiting for the imminent disaster uncovered some curious evidence you will find most helpful in your gardening.

1. Small children are by and large a far greater threat to gardens than any bug or disease.

2. The best reasons for using insecticides, organic or otherwise, only sparingly if at all on Two Acre Eden are fireflies. Their flickering beauty at dusk is worth more than all the strawberries, sweet corn, and cantaloupes in the world.

3. Aphids come and go as they damn well please. Neither chemical sprays, which are supposed to kill them, nor ladybugs, which are supposed to eat them, have much effect on their migrations.

4. Timing is a key factor in bug control, if you can figure out the key. Take corn earworms and borers, two of my favorite non-pets. Last year I planted Golden Cross Bantam three times about a week apart. The first to mature averaged about one worm to every two ears. And borers had tunneled into about half of the stalks (with little ill effect on the yield, by the way). But the worms did not touch the second planting. The third was infested but not as badly as the first. Naturally, my second planting is always the biggest. It matures between the two generations of worms.

5. Cats wreak more vengeance on the bird population than DDT ever did.

6. A *small* amount of acidulated fertilizer will not deplete your earthworm population, contrary to what some of the proponents of Pure Organics say. If you maintain a good mulch covering on your garden, you will have plenty of earthworms, even with a small application of inorganic fertilizers. But why use chemical fertilizers when the worms provide fertility in a much healthier form?

7. The only way to keep birds out of cherry trees is to hang a dozen birdcages in each tree with a cat in each cage. Or cut the tree down and store it in the garage for firewood.

8. Without sprays, you will get an increase in the praying mantis and ladybug populations in your garden. The advantage is that both bugs are beneficial. They eat other bugs. Besides, they're real characters to watch. Just as a mantis finally gets up enough energy to pounce on a bad bug, a bird comes along and pounces on the mantis. Moral: Don't expect too much help in bug control from the praying mantis.

9. If you mulch with a lot of fresh straw, grass clippings, or unrotted sawdust, you do *not* have to add some kind of nitrogen. Only if the unrotted mulch is incorporated into the soil will it use up soil nitrogen as it decays. In this event, add nitrogen or your sweet corn will look something like last year's cattails.

10. Living in tune with the rhythms of nature may sound farfetched, but it isn't. Even if you can practice it only on weekends, you'll live longer. My father called it, "Let's-go-sit-and-watch-the-river-awhile." And when I was a boy, we would. Maybe put a fishing line in the water so passersby would think we were normal. But the idea was just to sit there and absorb life. In later years I used to slip off to a particular stretch of the Minnesota River, go for a swim with the current, crawl up on a half-submerged log and melt in some very real way into the fabric of nature around me. Sometimes a muskrat would join me on the log, a turtle would float by, a deer would glide to the water's edge. But I was not consciously aware of these particular examples of life; only of a soft breeze and of Life ebbing and flowing. Now I have no stretch of river private enough or clean enough to swim in. I've shifted my exercises in Becoming Aware of Life to gardening in my Two Acre Eden.

Chapter 3

If the Bull Would
Throw You, Lie Down:
Heretical Horticulture,
Part I

Because I am going to hand out opinionated advice that may raise a few eyebrows in conventional gardening circles, I must qualify, first of all, what I'm going to say — give you the why before the what and how. By definition, gardening on a Two Acre Eden with the purpose of raising much of your own fresh, pure food can be Work. Also by definition, your homestead must meet its first reason for being: to provide you with a place of peace, beauty, and a modicum of contentment. In other words, a Two Acre Eden that does not provide time for a siesta in the hammock, a lazy walk down the lane, and a pattern of activities varied enough to prevent boredom, fails utterly.

To accomplish these seemingly contradictory goals I have adopted a philosophy that allows me to follow certain practices of a somewhat controversial nature. These methods do not necessarily apply to commercial farming (though it is too bad if they don't), and they definitely do not apply to the specialty gardener, for instance, the hobbyist who grows quality roses to win ribbons at flower shows or who spends all his spare time in a skilled and exacting art of growing exotic plants. In the first case, my methods are often impractical or impossible for large-scale commercial enterprises. In the second case, the gardener who tends to an acre or more, and plans to enjoy himself in the country besides, doesn't usually have the time for the exacting requirements of specialization.

The first secret of gardening on a large scale without becoming a slave is learning to work with nature, or letting nature do the work for you. The commercial gardener or farmer can't always do this. He finds himself forced by the vicissitudes of the market into conflict with nature. To make a profit, he must raise his crops to mature earlier than they normally would. He must assure his outlets a steady supply of standard produce. He must deliver food unblemished by bug or disease. He must fight nature right down to the goal line. The exotic plant grower is in conflict with nature from the start; the plants he chooses to grow aren't native to his area or climate, or will survive there only with the utmost care, skill, and culture. You, the owner of Two Acre Eden, do not have these problems — yours is simply to surround yourself with good food, beauty, and interesting activities.

First, you learn *what* to grow. The main reason everything does so well for the old, experienced gardener is simply because he has stopped trying to grow plants that for one reason or another wouldn't produce well for him. As the old gardener across the road from us puts it: "By the time you're 90 like me, you finally learn what plants to avoid if you had your life to live over." After 90 years, he learned the first commandment of ecology: Adapt to nature, don't try to control it down to the last limit of your ambitions.

As a gardener, you will go through stages where you try everything. If you're doing it for fun, splendid. But don't hang your hat on Brussels sprouts; cabbage is so much safer and easier, and the Savoy varieties are just as tender and delicately flavored. French shallots and Chinese snow peas are excellent means of one-upping a fellow gardener, but when it's all said and done, a young green scallion and a plate of fresh Little Marvel peas taste every bit as good and are twice as dependable.

Part of the fun of gardening is to try every new variety that comes along (or every old one you hear about). But don't rely on one of them for a main crop until it proves itself in your garden.

Nor should you expect much from crops not meant for your area. If you grow Florida Ninety strawberries in Minnesota, don't look for any sympathy when they don't produce well. I have a sister who insists on trying to grow blueberries in alkaline soil. She saturates the ground with aluminum sulfate and oak leaves, both of which make soil more acid. But her blueberry bushes never perform like they should. You just can't grow a long-season watermelon variety in Maine. I can't resist trying odd kinds of sweet corn. This year I grew Black Mexican, an ancient variety highly touted for its flavor. Since the kernels turn purple when fully mature, the ears make a nice touch in a fall centerpiece on the table. But the corn did not produce very well for me, and didn't taste any better or as well as other white corn like Silver Queen.

I see no wisdom in trying to grow fruits and vegetables out of their proper season on Two Acre Eden. You simply will not get much production out of everbearing strawberries in most parts of the country. Late-fall corn lacks taste. Extremely early varieties of melons seldom produce well or taste half as good as full-season varieties. Cold-weather crops like cabbage and lettuce planted in midsummer for a fall crop may or may not be successful, but they are really unnecessary. Full-season broccoli and cabbage will last until frost anyway. And who needs lettuce when endive and kale are at their peak? Everything has its season, and the wise gardener will recognize this and eat accordingly, freezing or canning the excess of each crop for off-season eating.

Most gardeners are tempted to plant early; there is status in having the first corn or the first tomato in the neighborhood. You will often pay for such foolishness. (See chapter 5.) In my clayish soil, I almost always get impatient and plant too early and then have to plant over or suffer along with a poor stand and sometimes stunted growth. I've had potatoes freeze, and I've had poor germination on even cold-weather crops like cabbage and peas. If you plant 60-day corn in cold ground, it will take 75 days to mature anyway. The temperature of the soil governs these things, not the instructions on the seed packet. For the 4 or 5 days you might gain with an earlier crop, you'd best wait until the soil is warmer. You've got a lot of work to do without doing it twice.

Accomplished gardeners are always starting seeds in the house in early spring, or in cold frames or hotbeds, then transplanting the seedlings to the garden after all danger of frost is past. Almost every gardening book devotes chapter upon chapter to the complexities of this operation. How to mix good starting soils, how to sterilize dirt to avoid "damping-off" disease, how to construct a hotbed or cold frame, and so on and on. You will find, if you don't take my word for it, that most of this work is unnecessary for noncommercial gardeners. If you have a normally decent garden soil and don't live in the Far North, where the growing season is extremely short, you can sow most, if not all, of your vegetable seeds directly in the ground. You won't have the earliest lettuce in the neighborhood, but the difference will be only slight. Besides, you can be eating dandelion greens, which come up all by themselves, while waiting for the lettuce to grow. Leeks need a long season to mature, and I should, according to the book, start mine inside to get a jump on the weather, but we happen to like our leeks better when only half mature, so I plant them right in the garden.

The tomato is the only vegetable I regularly start under cover for transplanting later. And I have direct-seeded tomatoes many times with good results, too. I start them early partly because tomatoes are so good with any meal, we like to have them as soon as possible, and partly because they are so easy to start.

I buy a box of Jiffy-7 Peat Pellets, those little wafers that swell into a peat pot when you sprinkle water on them.

I space them out in a seed flat on top of a couple of inches of vermiculite, a sterile, cheap growing medium. After the wafers swell into pots, I insert a couple of seeds in each one. There's a sufficient amount of plant food in each pot to last the plant until transplanting. I put the flat on top of the furnace until the seed germinates, then place it on a protected porch in front of a south window. Whenever the weather is warm enough, I set the flat outside (only an hour the first time or two, until the plants begin to harden off). When the soil is warm and frost is past, I set the peat pots right in the garden. No roots are disturbed, and I've never had damping-off problems.

I sometimes grow melons in flats too, but the ones I seed directly in the garden usually do as well as the transplants, and often better.

With fruit trees and ornamentals, I apply my same rule of thumb: I work with nature as much as possible, and don't do anything I don't have to do. Again the trick is learning what to avoid.

This kind of thinking has led me on a wild-goose chase for the perfect shade tree. The perfect shade tree is the one that grows fast and vigorously in any soil, yet requires no pruning. It has beautiful blossoms, which do not develop into seeds that fall to the earth and then spring up into a multitude of seedlings, nor grow into fruits which make an unsightly and rotting mess on the ground. The leaves of the perfect shade tree are a brilliant green in summer, then turn to various shades of gold and red in fall, then evaporate into the thin air. The perfect shade tree suffers from no diseases, is eaten by no bugs, has no roots to clog drains or raise humps up around its trunk to break mower blades. It does not litter the ground with dead branches, nor fall on your roof during windstorms.

In short, the perfect tree does not exist. Only imperfect ones, and some more imperfect than others. For instance in New Jersey, there is a law against planting Lombardy poplars. I congratulate the enlightened genius who pushed that one through the legislature. The tall, stately, fast-growing Lombardys — "standing like serene sentinels along your property line," as some misbegotten advertising poet put it—begin to die after about a dozen years of fast growth, and then they topple over onto your neighbor's property. Good Lombardys do not make good neighbors.

Though the wrath of the nursery industry descend upon me, I'd add a few more plants to the outlaw class. Like Osage orange. Like multiflora roses. At least no one sells Japanese honeysuckle anymore. It has already increased and covered the earth. But the multiflora rose business is hotter than ever, except in enlightened states where it has been banned. "A living fence, with beautiful, sweet-smelling blossoms; a haven for wildlife and birds." Yes. And unless you keep after it with brush killer and a hedge trimmer all the days of your life, it will turn your backyard into one vast brier patch.

There are other plants in the ornamental field that are out-and-out frauds. The Better Business Bureau can supply you with a list of nursery companies that the Postal Inspection Service claims have sold certain products by means of false advertising. Included is the ailanthus tree— "a fantastic supergrowing variety . . . soars roof high in only a few months." That of course is true. An easy way to tear down a building is to plant ailanthus in the cracks of the foundation and wait 10 years. Ailanthus is famous as the tree that grew in Brooklyn, and if Brooklyn were suddenly abandoned, in 40 years the ailanthus would turn it into an impenetrable forest.

Other products on the list include the "Gleditsia Tree," the "Robinia Tree" ("living torches, up to 3,000 blooms in a single day"), and the "Wonder Rose" ("up to 1,000 fresh new roses every 7 days").

Even with very respectable plants, experience soon teaches which ones to favor if you want to save yourself time and worry. To keep American boxwoods alive and happy, lots of people spray them well every year in May. But the bug that goes after them doesn't bother the English boxwoods at all. Sheer logic says switch to the English and save myself a spraying or two. The various types of taxus (yews) have, in my experience, fewer enemies than any other evergreen. They grow in sun or shade, take trimming well, and are handsome. Any future replacements I make in evergreen hedges or bushes are bound to be yews.

Birds like best to peck on red and yellow peaches. So grow white peaches. Or grow a red and two whites, the former for the birds, the latter for you. Birds gobble black sweet cherries faster than yellow ones. Grow yellows. Is it wise to raise hollies that freeze back every third winter if you can grow spruces that never do? Why grow a paper birch where a paper birch doesn't want to grow? Grow a gray birch. Or better yet, no birch at all, especially where the birch leaf miner turns them brown by June 1.

If a magnolia is not hardy in your area, it won't make you a good tree, no matter how pretty its picture looks in the catalog. To select the best tree for your lawn, go out in the woods near you, and see what kinds are doing best there. That's what you should grow. A pin oak, if native to your area, is just as beautiful as a golden chain tree and will last about 100 years longer.

A friend of mine, who has been living among the "savages" in the wilds of Zambia so long that he calls Africa home, visited us last week and taught me a lot about adapting to nature.

As I sprinkled rotenone on my eggplants, which were being perforated by the confounded flea beetles, he smiled and said: "An African would be too smart to raise something as bothersome or risky as that. Life is too short to waste time fighting nature unnecessarily. Who needs eggplant?"

I let that go.

A little later, I was sweating over some wood I should have chopped up to fit the fireplace last winter instead of now in the heat of summer.

"Africans would be too smart to do that," he observed again. "They are very tricky. They build a fire in the house in such a way that they can burn up a very long log and never have to cut it. They just stick one end in the flame and keep moving the log up as it burns. You never do work that nature will do for you."

In the evening, we were sitting in the house and a spider ran down the wall. I got him.

"We have a house spider in Zambia that everyone calls Charlie. Africans would be too smart to kill them. Charlies look ugly, but they control other bugs that you don't want around."

The conversation moved around to the problems of young people today, as it inevitably does, and everyone gave his or her opinion for the 500th time on the changing moral standards.

My friend, who was by now becoming obnoxious with his ethnic comparisons, opined that in the bush, teenage sex and related problems hardly exist. "Children are allowed to engage in promiscuous sexual relationships until they reach puberty. Nobody thinks anything of it. Soon after puberty, the girls get married. Surprisingly it works pretty well—at least, better than the American way. The kids do not develop psychological hang-ups. All your furor over premarital sex and so-called new morality would make the Bantu split his sides laughing. It's a different culture. They accept nature."

Before the week was over, my friend caught the flu. "Always happens when I come back," he explained. "We don't have much flu over there, and we get quite susceptible to it." He also claimed the Bushmen never get ulcers, rarely have bad teeth, and the school kids from the bush are every bit as quick and smart as any bunch of European or American children he knew.

I reminded him of malaria, tsetse fly, protein deficiency, and the Bushman's much shorter life span, all of which, among other things, keep these people very far from an idyllic life. Of course, he agreed. "But just as they can benefit from our technology, so we could benefit from their philosophy, or naturalism," he said. "Yet a civilization rarely makes this kind of selection. Now Africa is opting for technological civilization—all of it, and the end will be the same as in America—hearts that stop beating before their time and lungs black with factory smoke."

The main garden product of the particular section of Zambia where my friend lives is cassava root. From it, the people grind a meal which can be baked into bread and used in many other dishes. Africans have been growing cassava for centuries. Nothing much attacks it. Both soil and climate are favorable for its growth. The wisdom of tradition tells the Bantu: "You have your hands full staying alive in a fairly comfortable way. Don't take any more risks than you have to. Raise cassava. It is reliable. It will keep you alive. Learn many ways to cook it, and you will love it." And they do.

The apple has been popular in the United States, especially in pioneer times, for much the same reason. The apple tree can be depended upon to bear fruit 15 out of 20 years without the necessity of standing by "holding its hand" all summer. In many different soils and various zones of hardiness, the apple flourishes better than other fruits. As food, apples are versatile. There are specific apples to eat fresh, to store, to dry, to make pies, to make sauce, to make vinegar, to make cider and applejack.

My apple trees always produce without much help on my part. On the other hand, I must continually fuss with my peach trees. Either I am fighting bugs and worms or worrying that cold weather will kill the buds. Ecologically, I ought to stick to apples. As the African proverb says: "If the bull would throw you, lie down."

Chapter 4

Some of My Best Friends Are Night Crawlers: Heretical Horticulture, Part II

Once you have learned which plants you can grow successfully with the least amount of fuss and bother, all you have to do is treat the soil correctly and you will be a successful gardener, even if you were born and raised on Broadway. After all, you don't grow the plants; they grow themselves.

When you buy your seeds, directions on the packet or in your favorite magazine or catalog will invariably say: Plant on fertile, well-drained soil. That is advice? What the Sam Hill are you supposed to do if you don't have fertile, well-drained soil? Or, if you do, how do you keep it that way?

The whole life of a gardener is to be in love with soil. I am convinced that if man would learn to love and properly care for the top five inches of the earth's crust, the world would have only half the troubles it suffers today. If that sounds oversimplistic, you owe it to yourself as a genuine gardener to read some books on soil* or the history

*One of my favorites is *Man and His Earth* by George D. Scarseth (Ames, Iowa: Iowa State University Press, 1962).

of any civilization which has misused its soils.

Take a practical case. I don't know how many dis-illusioned suburbanites have come to me with the complaint that around their new houses the bulldozers have scraped away all the topsoil, and the only thing that will grow well on the hard clay left there is crabgrass.

If you are looking for a new home and if gardening is really important to you, be careful how you choose a new homesite. If you know a developer really well, he will confess that he doesn't make much money on the houses. He makes money on the lots. He pays, let us say, $5,000 an acre for the land, if he's lucky. He divides an acre into four or six or more lots, which he sells for $10,000 to $15,000 each. Of course he has terribly high expenses developing that land, but you can see there is some profit in it too.

But there are not many tracts anywhere in the world that nature ever intended to hold that many houses. So the developer must reshape the land. He tears up the sod that is on it, often tears down any trees growing there because they may stand below grade for drainage purposes. Often he must add soil to the lot, so that it is deep enough over bedrock to pass the septic-tank percolation test — a subterfuge that is seldom successful.

In some subdivisions where this practice of artifi-cially increasing the soil depth has been used, runoff from septic tanks is oozing up in the lawns. If you buy a place like this, budget out $2,000 to $3,000 that you are going to have to pay to hook up to the sewer when it comes through. If sanity prevailed in building and if 70 percent of Americans didn't insist upon living on 2 percent of the land, we'd have laws prohibiting small lots. This might automatically keep land prices more reasonable, and help prevent leapfrogging, helter-skelter development. Septic systems could continue to work beautifully in lieu of sewers and cut down drastically on stream pollution.

I am telling you all this not to criticize developers, who do the best they can usually, but simply to make you aware that, if your hobby is scratching in the ground, you want as much quality in your soil as you do in your house.

When you are thinking about buying a piece of ground, look at it before the bulldozers get there and try to keep track of where the topsoil goes. Look at the lot real well right after or during a late-winter rainstorm. You may notice that the lot has a low spot that turns into a pond after a rain. That spot will not make a good garden. The developer sometimes scoops such a spot out a little deeper, builds a basement in it, and a house on that, land-scapes it all, and everything looks nicely, nicely. But the basement may be wet for all eternity, even when efforts are made to grade the surrounding area to detour the water elsewhere—and grading usually means good-bye topsoil.

I can give you other reasons why you should avoid buying a new house in a new subdivision of less than one-acre lots (and even of less than two-acre lots), but sometimes you have no choice. If you can't afford enough land to protect yourself from man-made gardening disasters, then buy in an established area, not in a new subdivision. Such areas, if developed 50 or 100 years ago, have had any faults in the original development corrected by now in one way or another. They didn't have bulldozers 50 years ago, so they couldn't wreak havoc so easily.

As you drive along the highway, slow down, as the signs say, and look closely behind the houses of small villages you are passing through. Very often, these places are perfect for little Edens.

Behind the houses you will see small barns (sometimes big barns), gardens already laid out, fruit trees, and grape arbors, often an acre or more in size. All of which can be bought reasonably and are within close proximity to grocery stores and other services you need. Often, the city dweller seeking relief from the city shuns these spots, because they look like what he is trying to escape. He's wrong. Go visit some rural villages of under 5,000 population and look around. Your Two Acre Eden could be right there, under your nose.

Your other alternative is to buy your own spot in the country far enough from new developments that land prices aren't beyond your pocketbook. This way you can tell by looking what is hill and what is valley and what is swamp. The bulldozers haven't come yet.

If you are lucky enough to be able to buy your own acreage like this, approach its development with the eyes of the ecologist.

If you have a woodlot, leave it alone. A forest can take care of itself. You can clear brushy growth and mow around the big trees, or you can graze sheep in it and accomplish the same result. But then you have a park, not a wood. Let woods evolve into a climax of hardwoods, and harvest the big trees (if you really need the money) as they begin to show signs of dying of old age.

If you have a swamp, you may possibly be able to drain it and turn it into a meadow of reed canary grass. But why not leave it as a swamp? In exchange for a few extra mosquito bites, you will get a daily insight into the myriad forms of wild animals and plants that are part of the ecology of a swamp.

Put your house in a protected spot shielded from prevailing cold winds. A split-level set into an east-facing hillside gives you a lower floor that's always cool in summer and warm in winter. Or build on the east side of your woods—the trees make a natural windbreak. Either way you will save on fuel. And winter days outside will be more pleasant—an advantage you can't appreciate unless you've worked around a farmstead in January.

Don't build a house in the middle of a dense forest. Your house will always be dark and damp if you do, and after a couple of years you'll develop a sort of claustrophobia and wish your windows looked out on clean sweeps of open lawn.

If you intend to build a barn for livestock don't build it too close to the house, or you may be bothered by flies in the kitchen.

If you plant an orchard, put the trees on a hillside if you can. The reason for this is that air "flows" just about like water, and in cold weather, cold air tends to run down-hill, seeking the lowest level. On a cold night the movement of air on the hillside can raise the temperature there by a degree or two, just enough to keep tender fruit buds and blossoms from freezing. If you have a north-facing slope this one is best for fruit trees, oddly enough. On the north slope, the rays of the winter sun do not strike directly. On a southern exposure, the winter sun can warm up a tree so that the sap begins to rise fast even on a February afternoon, and the buds begin to swell. Then, if the temperature plummets close to zero that night, the buds can freeze easily, and sometimes the bark on the tree will split. Furthermore, the warm, early spring sun can induce a tree on a protected southern exposure to start growing sooner and blossom right when frost danger is greatest. On a north slope, blossoming may be held back a few days more until frost has past.

This lesson in winter hardiness and microclimates is frequently misunderstood by gardeners. Even on a cold winter day, the temperature on the "sheltered" side of a house or wall may rise to 90 degrees or more when the sun is shining. If this happens in an area where night temperatures are severe, a "protected" southern exposure is a poor place to plant a tender plant like a holly. Plant your holly on the north side of your house, and you will have better luck. The reason you put burlap coverings over boxwood is to protect them from winter sun just as much as winter wind. The reason you spread mulch over strawberries after the ground freezes, is not to protect the plants but to prevent alternate thawing and freezing of ground, which heaves the plants out. Coldness alone seldom winter-kills plants.

If you do not have good topsoil to work with, don't despair. You can create good garden soil out of almost any plot that is not pure rock or the bottom of a swamp. It just takes time.

The thing that makes topsoil different from subsoil is the amount of humus in it. Humus is decomposed organic matter, and organic matter is any kind of plant tissue that can decay in the ground and return to it the nutrients originally taken up by that plant. Organic matter is what

good garden soil is all about. It both enriches the ground
and improves soil tilth.

In the fall, plow under all the grass clippings, mulch,
manure, and other organic matter you can get hold of.
Then plant the plot to a green-manure crop like rye. Lime
heavily, except where you want to grow acid-loving plants.

In the spring, plow or rotary till under the rye after
it grows awhile. Top-dress rock phosphate and potash or,
if you must use acidulated fertilizers, commercial 0-20-20
sparingly. As you plant your seeds, add a small amount of
nitrogen fertilizer, preferably something organic. When the
plants have a good start, lay on the mulch six inches thick—
compost, manure, grass clippings—again, anything
organic. Spread that thickly—the mulch will smother out
most weeds. And for conserving moisture, mulch is almost
as good as irrigation.

Repeat the process every year, and you will eventually create new topsoil. And after several years, the ground
will be so rich, you won't have to add extra fertilizer at all.

Mulching is, for me, a tremendous time-saver. I can
state unequivocally that on my schedule and with my
extensive gardens, I could not keep the weeds under control without it. In fact, mulch-gardening has so many
benefits in so many ways, I have attempted to use it in
place of all cultivation, with some notable successes. For
instance, when I turn under a patch of sod or heavy cover
crop, I am faced with an immediate problem. My little
rotary tiller simply can't handle sod satisfactorily. I've not
found any rotary tiller that will. One year I hired a man
to tear up a piece of lawn with a big, tractor-driven tiller,
and even after two trips over the ground, he still left me
with unmanageable lumps of sod all over the surface. Nor
will small garden tractors with small conventional plow
blades turn sod under adequately. You need a big brute
of a tractor and a 12-inch, 2-bottom plow to get the job
done. Lacking that, I was forced to spend many an October
and November evening spading up relatively huge areas by
hand. (Any area is huge when you are hand-spading
in the dark.)

I had a problem, and the solution only came to me in the fall, after I had set out my blueberry and raspberry plots. That spring, I had dug narrow strips in the lawn, lifted the thick sod out of the strip, and set the plants in the soil underneath. I hated to lose the organic matter the sod represented if turned under, but with my equipment and a very limited amount of time to get the bushes planted, I had little choice. All summer I had to fight weeds that grew in the strip of ground, and the grass encroached on the plants and robbed them of water and nutrients. The raspberries and blueberries grew with little vigor. I knew I had to remove the sod between the berry rows. Since there were four rows of bushes over 100 feet long, and the sod growing between the rows was 8 feet wide, that meant a lot of spading.

About that time I began reading articles by Ruth Stout in *Organic Gardening and Farming* magazine about complete mulch-gardening with no cultivation at all. Why not just cover all that sod with a foot of dead leaves? Wouldn't that kill the grass, smother weeds, and eventually rot into compost?

My wife talked the street department of our village into bringing us our first big truckload of leaves. The pile they left was not the fluffy mound you rake up, but a solid, ground-up mass that as a layer of mulch would last a long time. In fact, I was afraid the leaves were so matted together that they might seal out rain.

Instead of spading those dark November evenings away, I piled the leaves thickly between the rows, being very careful not to pile them too high right next to the berry bushes. The next spring, after the weather warmed up, I raked the leaves up close to the bushes to smother out the little weeds that already were starting to grow there. That was all the work there was to it.

All summer the leaves kept rotting away. The only weeds that could push their way through were a few dandelions, which I pulled out by hand. The berry bushes, especially the blueberries, grew with absolutely marvelous vigor. In the driest weather, I could dig down under the rotting leaves and find unbelievably moist soil. And huge earthworms by the hundreds. By fall, the plot was like a forest floor without trees. On top was an inch of dry leaves. Then an inch of moist leaf mold, then two inches of moist soil where the thick sod had already turned into humus.

Now each year, I simply add more leaves on top. Around the raspberries, I scatter a little lime or wood ashes to counteract the acidity of the leaves; nothing need be put around the blueberries, which thrive on acid soil. I cannot imagine a richer loam than I have developing there. And nature did almost all the work. I don't even have to build a compost pile. The leaves compost very well in their thick layer. I can even bury small dabs of garbage from the kitchen under the leaves. No mess, no smell, and it soon rots away.

One spring, I started another new plot of garden in the sod. I tried to plow under the grass with an old tractor and an even older two-bottom plow. I did such a poor job that I was barely able to scratch together enough loose soil to make mounds in which to plant my melons, squash, and gourds. My plot looked as if someone had been bombing it for three weeks.

Then I ran across a guy who had just finished mowing nearly three acres of lawn. He had even raked the grass clippings into piles. Could I have them? Bless you, crazy man, take them all.

I scattered the clippings ten inches deep over my bomb craters and rolls of dislodged sod. Nothing more was done to the plot all summer except a little hand weeding around the mounds when the melon and squash seedlings first came up. By late fall, the sod chunks under the mulch had all rotted away, and the loose soil could be easily worked by my rotary tiller the next spring, if I wanted to use it.

I say "if," because I actually planted potatoes there, just dropping them on top of the ground and piling another layer of mulch on top of them. All I had to do was pull back the mulch and pick up the potatoes.

Plastic mulches are very handy in the garden too,

especially if you cannot get a sufficient supply of leaves, grass clippings, old hay or straw. I know a gardener with a reputation for having the earliest direct-seeded vegetables in his neighborhood. What he does is to leave one strip of black plastic mulch on the garden over winter. In early spring, the black plastic absorbs the heat of the sun and warms the ground under it a little faster than other soil. A week or so before anyone else can get into the garden, he rolls back the plastic. The ground is free of weeds and so friable it dries quickly, and he can work it up easily with a hand cultivator.

The only objection I have to plastic mulches is that they don't add organic matter to the soil. On the other hand, the main disadvantage of thick organic mulches is that they prevent the ground from warming up quickly in the spring.

There are two solutions to this latter problem. One is that quite often the mulch will have rotted away by spring, especially if you use grass clippings. The second solution is to rake the mulch away from the immediate spots where you intend to set out plants or seeds in hills.

I also found at first that the mulch harbored mice and shrews, which ate some of my produce. The first year I grew muskmelons on mulch, the shrews ate holes in some of them. I solved that problem in two ways. First, we acquired two cats, and for a while they were averaging at least one shrew a day. Second, I tried an idea passed on to me by another melon grower. I cut plastic one-gallon milk jugs in half lengthwise, and set each ripening melon in one of these containers, being careful not to tear the melon stem when I lifted it. I punched a hole in each container so rain water could get out. For some reason, most animals that like melons won't bother them in these containers. And the melon is less apt to rot on the bottom since it is no longer in direct contact with the ground.

I still work the soil up with my rotary tiller for planting row crops like corn and beans. But I have one plot of ground that has not been disturbed by plow, tiller, rake, or hoe for three years. It has been perpetually covered with layers of grass clippings and manure. I merely dig small holes through the mulch to set tomato plants the first year, then melons the next year, then eggplants. No cultivation, few weeds, and the most vigorous vegetables I have ever seen.

Everyone ought to have a list of rules for gardening. Here are mine:

Rule 1. Violate all rules at least once, just for the heck of it. You may discover something new. I planted 12 peach seeds, from which grew 12 seedlings that every orchardist and nurseryman told me would be "no damn good." Only grafted true varieties from nurseries (cost: over nine dollars each) produce good peaches. Well, my seedlings are fun and free. Two of them have good peaches and have grown twice as fast and produced sooner than the good nursery trees I bought the same year. Another has charming red leaves that make it the prettiest ornamental on the place.

It is very stupid to lay down hard and fast rules about gardening. I consider myself an expert on strawberries. Especially eating them. One day I got a call from the wife of a good friend of mine. It was August — an extremely hot, dry August. Said she: "A neighbor of ours is tearing up an old strawberry bed, and he says I can have all the plants I want to start my own patch. Can I start it now?"

I sighed in relief. Finally, someone had asked me a question I could answer with some authority. "No," I said pompously. I told her one thing I had learned was that gardening has so many ifs and buts about it, that a person who wants to grow some berries to eat has no business being just half safe. There was only a small chance that her berry patch would make good under such conditions. She'd be much smarter to wait until spring, buy some good, virus-free plants, and do it right.

"But that would mean waiting a whole year more for berries, wouldn't it? If these grow, they'll make some shortcake next year, won't they?"

"Yeah, if. Do you know which plants to transplant?

Do you know what a first-year runner looks like?"

We kept on discussing the subject, during which I paraded a clever line of strawberry knowledge. But I could tell from the tone of her voice that the instincts of womanhood were holding out against all reason.

"Well, if you insist on stirring around in the dust and risking sunstroke, go ahead," I surrendered. "Just remember, I told you so."

She sure did remember. She invited us over next June for strawberry shortcake. And smiled benignly at every spoonful I ate.

The only rule I hold to for the home gardener is to do your own thing. I'm tempted to believe that plants have emotions, and that they know when someone loves them. I feel this way mostly because people who love plants begin to think like plants and they just sort of surmise eventually, what a plant wants. If they were plants, that's what they'd want.

So if you believe in planting root crops in the dark of the moon, plant in the dark of the moon. If you think cucumbers should be planted when the sign of the zodiac is descending from the arms to the legs, then by all means, do it. I've always wanted to plant by the zodiac myself, but have never been able to find three true believers who could agree on precisely what was the dark and what was the light of the moon. Or exactly when a certain sign of the zodiac was in command. It always depended on a subjective decision. You can never catch a believer of astrology in error. There are always too many alternate answers. And finally, when there is no other excuse, he — or she — says simply: "Well, I read the sign wrong."

Rule 2. Most of the pruning rules handed out to home gardeners have application only or mostly to commercial operations. The noncommercial fruit grower should read as little as possible about pruning and obey only one rule: Prune as little as you can get away with. Anybody can figure out that you should remove dead and wounded branches. Do not allow weak crotch angles of less than 45 degrees on fruit trees to develop. Other than that, there is really no one right way to prune anything. Styles go in and out of vogue. A grapevine can be pruned "correctly" several ways or trained to climb a tree or any kind of arbor your imagination can dream up. Up until this year, I always followed the old advice that if you prune suckers from tomato plants, you will get fewer but larger tomatoes. And conversely, if you don't pinch suckers, you get more but smaller tomatoes. Now I have found that if the ground is rich enough and moisture adequate, you don't have to prune suckers or stake the plants, and you can still get bushels of very large tomatoes indeed.

Severe pruning is the secret to growing the largest fruit in town, but it takes know-how. Pinch off all runners from a strawberry plant, and you will get mammoth berries. If you allow only two melons to grow on a plant of a naturally large cantaloupe variety, the 'loupes may get as large as watermelons. One of my peach trees had only one peach on it a few years ago; it ripened to the size of a softball. The lesson in all severe pruning however is apparent: You can't get very far down the road with one peach, even one the size of a basketball.

Rule 3. The seed companies have hybridized just about everything except hoe handles. Hybrid seed is considered the greatest horticultural invention since the potato. However, its benefits redound as much to the commercial grower and the seed company as to a Two Acre Eden man. It surprises even farmers sometimes to find out that open-pollinated corn is still being grown and sold in a few places. Good growers consistently get yields over 100 bushels to the acre with it, and farmers who use the corn to fatten cattle and hogs think it is more nutritious.

In the vegetable kingdom, the advantages of hybrid seed are thus enumerated: more vigor; better taste; even maturity; standard size, shape, and color; less susceptibility to the vagaries of weather, insects, and disease. Perhaps. Hybrid vegetables do mature more evenly to a more or less standard shape, size, and color, which is why the commercial market likes them, but it is a matter of know-how whether they grow more vigorously. For the small gardener, a patch of corn that ripens all at the same time is not necessarily an advantage. An old, open-pollinated variety that ripens ears over a longer period of time may be ideal for the family that wants a few ears to eat every day. The hybrids may germinate better and yield better usually, but don't expect miracles just because you plant new F_1 generation wonder seed.

Hybrid seed, I want to repeat, is generally speaking better than nonhybrid. I merely want to inform you, as I frequently will in this book, that there are alternatives to modern technology. Somehow, it makes me uneasy when I see all farmers and gardeners become so dependent on seed companies for their seed. It goes against my independent nature. You cannot save seed from your hybrid varieties to plant the next year. Each year you must go back to the seed breeder and buy more hybrid seed. If you try to plant seed from a hybrid you grow in your garden, you get nothing much that's worthwhile except some odd throwback to the parent stock from which the hybrid came. Older, open-pollinated varieties reproduce themselves.

When I originally propounded that philosophy, proponents of hybrids pooh-poohed loudly. Then several months later, southern corn blight ran rampant through the country's commercial cornfields, gravely threatening the 1970 crop. Without getting technical about the whole thing here, the reason the blight ruined so much corn was traced directly back to the way hybrid seed companies were crossbreeding corn hybrids. That's not a criticism; they were coming up with very excellent seed. But since they were all following each other down the time-tested way, run sheep run, almost all the corn planted in 1970 came from about the same parent stocks and was not resistant to the new strain of southern blight. Standardization, the seductive mistress of the commercial market, brought considerable ruination.

One immediate effect, when it became known that there might be at least a 10 percent loss in the crop, was that seed companies began to recall their 1971 seed list prices. They thought there simply wasn't going to be enough seed resistant to the blight for 1971, and farmers were going to pay dearly for it. At the same time, there sat a stubborn old cuss I know out in Iowa who dared to be different. He had been raising open-pollinated corn for years and making money on it, and his corn was resistant to the blight. He had his own seed for 1971, thank you kindly.

Rule 4. When you are short on space, interplanting and successive planting are gardening techniques that you should learn.

Mostly you have to learn on your own too. Experience will teach you many tricks. I plant a row of lettuce between the two broccoli rows. By the time the lettuce is past eating stage, the broccoli has grown up and filled the space. If you grow vine plants — sweet potatoes, melons, cucumbers — next to early corn, the corn will be finished as soon as the vines reach it. The vines can then spread through the cornstalks — you can cut the stalks down if they cast too much shade. Successive planting simply means you double-crop an area. When early peas are finished, turn them under and plant fall crops: kale and endive. When the strawberry season is over, I quickly tear up the plot (around July 1) and plant my late corn. Employing practices like these make your garden twice as big as it really is.

Rule 5. Laziness is next to godliness. If you keep weeds down in June, you can let a few grow in August. They will scatter seed that may keep you busy next June, but in August the gardener needs time in a hammock to dream about what a wonderful garden he is going to have next year.

Rule 6. A fall vegetable garden produces much better in books than it does in the soil.

Rule 7. To dream about having a greenhouse is better than owning one. Ditto a swimming pool.

Rule 8. Despite all advice to the contrary, some root crops can be "stored," most years, right in the ground where they are growing until January. In fact, this April, we dug up small carrots planted last summer, about half of which were perfectly preserved and edible.

Rule 9. Finally, the more experience you gain in gardening a Two Acre Eden, the more you will realize that, in the final analysis, nature is not a mother or a friend. Adapting yourself to the ways of nature is a truce, a compromise, a necessary condition of survival. You do not commune with nature, you outfox her. All she really wants is our decaying bones to make compost for the forested jungle that she could turn America into in 100 years, if no one stopped her.

Chapter 5

My Tomato Is Bigger
than Your Tomato;
or, My Peas Are Up,
Are Yours?

Gardeners lie as wantonly as fishermen. One of the more hypocritical whoppers they like to perpetuate is that gardening is a relaxing leisure-time activity away from the rat-race competition of doing unto others before they do it unto you. At every opportunity men of the hoe repeat this myth to each other with owlish solemnity. They each hope the others will believe it and thereby be lulled to a complacency that will mean defeat in next year's race for the biggest, earliest tomato in town.

Every spring I used to endure this little ritual: As the snow melts away from my garden plot and I wait helplessly for drier weather, I hear good friend and neighbor Fred approaching. I can hear him because he is whistling between his teeth in a most irritating manner. He is whistling between his teeth because he has some triumphant news he wants me to be the first to hear. "Hey, Logsdon, my peas are up. Are yours?"

I try to pretend he doesn't exist, but the whistling through the teeth persists. Fred has a plot of ground on the warm, south side of his house that must be underlain with gravel all the way to China. The soil there dries out and warms up a good two weeks before my glacial plots do and Fred, faithful to customs that his family must have brought over from the old country, somehow manages to plant peas on Saint Patrick's Day—unusual for Zone V. He often has to replant in early April, but even then, he always has peas up before I do. I hate him.

The underlying truth is that gardening is but a thinly disguised exercise in gamemanship. The human animal is not happy unless it is conniving to beat his or her fellows to the punch. If he can't do it by way of bank account, or on the gridiron, or behind an executive desk, there is always the garden. The guy who makes a point of observing that his tomatoes are bigger than your tomatoes is father of the boy who says his dad is tougher than your dad.

Well, I'm a human animal, and I had my fill of Fred's whistling, if not his peas. One year I decided to fix his wagon good. On a Sunday in the fall when he was not home, I borrowed a tractor with a scoop on the front and disced out a patch of ground directly south of my garage (and out of Fred's over-the-backyard-fence view), hauled in a foot or so of rotted sawdust and sand, mixed it together, and then pushed the topsoil back over it. I hoped the bed would dry and warm in spring as quickly as Fred's. Just to be sure, I spread all my precious compost over the area. The soil looked so rich I felt I could root a baseball bat in it.

The next spring I bought a package of an extra early, extra hardy "smooth" pea. (The ordinary, wrinkled pea seed varieties have much higher quality but will not endure cold, wet soil as well.) The variety was appropriately named "Alaskan." On March 15, I poked holes in my pea patch and dropped in seed. I don't think the frost was completely out of the ground yet. Then I went back in the house to watch Fred and practice whistling through my teeth. It snowed on Saint Patrick's Day, and Fred could not plant until around March 28, after three days of quite warm weather. I raked the snow off my pea patch and was sure, tee-hee, that with the warm weather my peas had sprouted faster than his.

Sure enough, that proved to be true, and though the temperature hovered around 55 degrees F. for the next two weeks, in sheltered microclimates like mine, those hardy peas struggled up through the soil while Fred's plot remained dormant.

April 16 in eastern Pennsylvania that year was a glorious day, as I well remember it. I don't know if the weather was glorious or not, but my peas were two inches tall and Fred's were just pushing through the soil. It was time for Fred's annual put-down, so I stationed myself dutifully by my pea patch and pretended to be hoeing weeds.

Sure enough, the old whistler came around the corner of the house, his hat cocked at a debonair angle, his step jaunty. I kept hoeing. The whistling was right behind me. The whistling stopped. A throat cleared. I kept hoeing—and started whistling through my teeth. When I finally turned to him, he was still staring abjectly at my peas. "Hi, ole' buddy," I sang out gaily. "Say, you don't look so well. Nice peas, aren't they. Yours up yet?"

I didn't see Fred until midsummer, when he showed up bearing two ripe tomatoes when mine were only blossoming.

I have never (yet) gotten into the Great Tomato Race (GTR) but two other gardeners I know brought refinement to this game unsurpassed in the Western world. I shall call them Dork and Doogal, but the rest of the story I need embellish only a little.

Dork and Doogal are both avid gardeners who moved to the same rural, southern Indiana suburb when they retired—Dork from Louisville, Kentucky, and Doogal from Cincinnati, Ohio—and so perhaps there was a built-in rivalry from the very beginning. Both had been successful, competitive businessmen in their chosen professions, and neither had known much in the way of failure during their working lives, nor had much experience in playing second fiddle. They started gardening over the hedge from each other, as retired executives are wont to do, and as one year led to another and one tomato to another, a keen feeling of competition stealthily crept into their friendly relationship. Year I of GTR was all sweetness and light. Dork raised two bushels of Big Boys and Doogal two bushels of old-fashioned Marglobes. They shared information; they tasted each other's tomatoes. "Yes, Dork, your Big Boys certainly are bigger tomatoes," agreed Doogal graciously. "Yes, Doogal, your Marglobes do have a taste my Big Boys can't be compared with," agreed Dork in return.

In Year II of GTR, Dork tried some Early Giants and Doogal tried Big Boys. The Early Giants weren't all that much larger than the Big Boys, but they *were* earlier, a fact Dork mentioned more than once. Dork opined that possibly the black plastic mulch ($4.95 per roll) he had laid down had absorbed more heat from the sun and by warming the soil hastened maturity a little.

In Year III of GTR, Doogal did not appear at the garden store to buy plants as he customarily did. Dork missed him there, and wondered. He might have wondered even more if he knew that Doogal had purchased a 48-inch, plant light and growing unit ($49.95) and was growing his own plants. His plants were already larger than the ones Dork purchased at the nursery. They were varieties touted for being extra early.

Dork came up with an innovation of his own. He staked his tomatoes (6 fancy "tomato towers" cost $14.95, and he bought 18) and pruned them to only a few evenly spaced clusters as the plants grew. Doogal, confident with his early-started plants, was content to grow his tomatoes on mulch once again without pruning. The upshot was that while Doogal had ripe tomatoes sooner, Dork had big, beautiful, softball-size fruit so much showier than Doogal's that the latter's GTR victory was rendered meaningless.

By Year IV of GTR, both contestants cast aside all efforts to disguise the game they were playing. "By God, I'll show him who can grow big tomatoes," Doogal fomented to his wife. "By God, I'll show him who can grow early tomatoes," Dork sputtered, likewise to his beloved. Doogal bought a $175 indoor plant-growing unit that made Dork's little outfit look like small potatoes, and in it he grew eight different varieties, all known for large size. Dork counterattacked by buying two more of the small units and filling the trays with ten different varieties, all known for early ripening. Each bought light and moisture meters ($20) for monitoring potting soils indoors and soil thermometers ($13) for checking outdoor soil. Dork purchased a $13 mister, and Doogal responded with a $75 drip-irrigation system. Dork decided he needed a packaged growing kit containing high-powered fertilizer, labels, plastic marking pen, potting mixtures, and peat pots, all for only $11.95. Doogal, seeing a chance to score one for organic gardening, purchased $45 worth of dried manure. The battle lines were drawn.

The outcome, as you may have guessed, was the opposite of the year before. Dork grew mostly earlier tomatoes, but Doogal, learning to prune suckers cleverly, grew bigger ones. As for taste, Doogal said he could even tell the better taste of manure-fertilized tomatoes in catsup made from them. Dork made catsup from his chemically fertilized tomatoes and challenged Doogal to a Blatz-like test. In disguised bottles, each tasted his own brand and his competitor's. Dork picked Doogal's over his own, and Doogal picked Dork's. Both wives stuck with Blatz and tried to pretend they were not married to idiots.

The contest would have ended in a draw that year except that by some quirk of genetics, one of Doogal's extra large tomatoes was pink enough to be called nearly ripe on the same day that Dork's earliest tomato ripened. Clearly, as Doogal insisted, Year IV of GTR belonged to him. The definition of victory had now been established. To win at GTR you had to grow the biggest *and* the firstest.

For Year V of GTR, Dork located a rare Japanese tomato called Hippo Dawn, which in oriental circles was rumored to be the largest early tomato of all. Seeds were $1.25 each. Meanwhile, Doogal ran across a brief reference in the horticultural literature alluding to a quaint variety from Belgium known in translation as Huge June, six seeds for $7.50.

Hippo Dawn and Huge June did not take well to American climate and the few small, late fruits that did grow tasted somewhat like cucumbers. Back to the drawing board for Dork and Doogal—in the meantime, their wives were buying tomatoes at the local roadside stand.

In Year VI of GTR, Dork and Doogal both started plants in early February, though both denied doing so. Dork moved blooming plants to the garden on May 10, since they no longer fit in the indoor growing units and were sprawling all over the living room. Doogal, believing Dork knew something he didn't, transplanted on May 11. On May 12, a killing frost abruptly ended the careers of what might have been the Earliest, Biggest Tomatoes Ever, except for a few that the wives had covered with sheets. Hot caps ($3.75 per 20) were too small to fit over the plants. Though alive, the sheet-protected plants turned yellow blue and remained stunted until June. Fortunately, the roadside stand had plenty of tomatoes to buy in midsummer.

By Year VII of GTR the two combatants had perfected such intricate and sophisticated methods to grow tomatoes that they had time for only three plants each. Dork pruned his to only one tomato per cluster and three clusters per plant to get the biggest possible fruits. Doogal after a little thought, decided to go for broke. He allowed only one tomato to develop on each of his three plants.

Such tomatoes you have never seen. They threatened to rival cabbages in size. All three of them. The question of the hour: Will their stems hold? Visitor after visitor was forced to walk by the plants and were not invited into the house until they had oooohed and aaaaahed sufficiently for the other contestant to hear, across the hedge.

Just as the tomatoes were ripening to ponderous red globes (at a cost of about $37.50 each, Doogal figured), a rainstorm swept through town. The sudden increase in soil moisture cracked Doogal's three prize fruits. Cracked is hardly the word. They literally exploded. All that was left were three fistfuls of juice oozing from the dangling split skins. Dork's fruit merely cracked, but the weight of the nine fruits—three per plant—broke the plants over in the wind despite stake ties, and the stems stripped loose.

So ended the Great Tomato Race, with a final score

of 0 to 0. Fortunately, the wives had started growing tomatoes, so there were some to eat after all. According to the wives, but denied by the husbands, Dork actually won the contest in a manner of speaking. When both men went to the garden the morning after the storm, Doogal threw one of his exploded tomatoes at Dork and missed. Dork returned the volley with his own fallen gems and plastered Doogal all over the back.

The moral of this story is that the Jeb Stuarts of the garden who want to get the firstest with the mostest, often end up the lastest with the leastest.

On Two Acre Eden, there is not much sense in trying to beat the season or the neighbors by making a garden at the first crack of spring. All those old folkloric traditions about planting potatoes on Good Friday, or peas on Saint Patrick's Day, or corn when oak leaves are as big as squirrel ears probably have their time and place on the scale of climate and frost zone, but the only sure rule is to plant when the soil is warm enough to germinate the seed. A soil temperature of 55 degrees F. is the bare minimum (and not at all satisfactory unless warmer weather immediately follows) for "cold weather" seeds like peas, potatoes, rye, wheat, oats, and cole crops. Warm-weather vegetables like sweet corn, beans, melons, tomatoes, eggplants, and peppers won't do any appreciable growing until the soil warms well above 60 degrees F.

Whenever the vegetative part of the plant is to be eaten, the secret of obtaining sweet, tender, lush vegetables is to grow the plant as fast as possible. That is, don't let the plant slow down in growth, once it has started its surge toward maturity. Cold weather slows and temporarily stunts the growth of vegetables, even if they do manage to germinate and begin growth. Anything you gain from early planting is lost—in time and in taste. The best example of that is asparagus. Since it is a perennial, it comes up each year when it feels like it. Asparagus is no smarter than impatient gardeners, and it will often leap partway out of the ground in that earliest spell of warm weather, then sit there with the return of cold weather, shivering.

When the weather warms again, it resumes growth, but when you eat spears that have suffered that kind of stress they are hard rather than succulent, bland rather than tasty.

If you plant beans in too big a hurry, stress from slow initial growth may not show up in the taste of the ultimate beans, but then again you may not get enough to taste at all. The bean comes up and, while shivering there waiting for the coming of more warm weather, is attacked by snail and slug and flea beetle and who knows what all. Without the ability to withstand and recover from such attacks, the first true leaves are eaten away, the cotyledons turn yellow, then brown, then so long, it's been good to know you. To counter these depredations, gardeners turn to an arsenal of chemicals and whine about the failure of organics.

Rapid growth of vegetables started in hot weather and kept well watered can be phenomenal. For example, observe watermelons and cantaloupes. In the North, many gardeners insist that these plants should be started early, indoors if necessary, so that they can get a full season of growth to mature sweetly. I have said the same thing, probably in this book, and to a certain extent it's true. But I have also learned that in really good soil with adequate rainfall, you can sow seed directly in the garden for even a relatively long-season watermelon like Charleston Grey, and almost any cantaloupe, *as late as June 1,* and still mature high-quality fruits. Plants started indoors will generally have *a few* melons earlier, but the direct-seeded plants will invariably be healthier and faster growing and yield more melons a little later. One day the plants seem to be way behind schedule, just beginning to vine out and blossom. Then they take off, with vines growing a foot a day, or more. Suddenly you see cantaloupes the size of walnuts. In just a few days, they're full size. I've seen Charleston Grey watermelons grow from fist size to football size in a week. And these same watermelons I no longer worry about even if they are setting fruit a little late. I've found that a watermelon can finish maturing even in September after *light* frosts have browned the leaves but have not killed the vines. I've eaten good watermelons out of the garden in November.

The best antidote for the early gardening fever is to take a vacation during those first balmy spring days, as far away from your tiller as you can get. The second way is to develop a perennial food garden that comes early without planting. Asparagus, rhubarb, perennial onions, and dandelions from the yard are the mainstays of this no-work garden. We have a patch of what we call nest onions, so named from the clusters of bulblets that form at the tips of the plants. These begin to grow almost as soon as the snow melts and are good until warm weather makes them too strong. Shallots are another hardy perennial, and we have learned that leeks will often overwinter for early eating. In addition we eat last year's carrots, left right in the ground until April. Sometimes the tops of the roots rot a little before then, but these can be cut off, still leaving plenty of good carrot. Kale will also overwinter, except in the coldest parts of the country, and provide a spring meal or two before going to seed. And, of course, there're always parsnips.

About the time your asparagus begins to play out, your peas should be coming along. Unless, of course, you've been playing the Jeb Stuart role too hard.

Chapter 6

An Ode to Horse Manure and Other By-Products Called Waste

The folk belief that a plaster of fresh cow dung (why is it you must write dung, but can't write what everyone says? They're both four-letter words meaning exactly the same thing) would help a cut was laughed into fantasyland, then damned into oblivion as suicidal. Putting dirt on a cut would lead to lockjaw and death, said the righteous.

But now that science is beginning to catch up with itself, researchers are slow to laugh at anything. Cow manure does indeed contain healing elements — certain essential protein substances, trace minerals, and vitamin B_{12} — manufactured in the cow's stomach. Science has merely put the elements in technological form.

Did you know where vitamin B_{12} was discovered? In chicken litter. Of course, the chickens knew it was there all the time, but because hens are so stupid and men are so smart, they've never been credited.

Commercial poultrymen, because of the demands of market economy, had been increasing the sizes of their flocks (and still are) in order to make a profit. They had, in the best view of "modern" husbandry, made great efforts to keep the houses into which chickens were jammed sterile and clean, to keep "germs" out. But the more they cleaned and disinfected, the more prone to some diseases and cannibalism the chickens became.

Then one day, some lazy farmer didn't clean out the old bedding in the chicken coop. God bless lazy people. He didn't clean it out the next year either—just continued to spread fresh straw on top. Behold, cannibalism, for which he had been spending money on various foolish preventives, disappeared from the flock. He hadn't changed feeding formulas. The only difference was all that litter, and the hens, he noticed, kept scratching in it and finding something there to eat.

And so it came to pass that chickens told men about B_{12}, and poultrymen all over the world began to let chicken litter compost itself in the coop. The only requirement was that the litter had to remain dry. Bacteria then began working away in it and out of defecation came health.

Of course, the huge commercial poultry houses today often keep chickens in individual cages and supply the necessary vitamins and protein in the feed. The economics of moving manure are such that for really big operations, litter-raising chickens won't pay. Whether or not you agree with their methods, you have to admit that they have kept chicken meat within reach of every family's budget.

The purpose of bringing this little story up is to put in proper perspective what we have been calling wastes, rubbish, garbage, offal, and manure.

Either we must adopt a new attitude toward waste, or, as ecologists and city planners are warning, we will bury ourselves in it. Wastes must be seen as a natural part of the life cycle and food chain; decay is a necessary prelude to life. And if man has, in his infinite wisdom, invented brilliant materials like plastic that will not decay in a suitable length of time, then he must reuse them or go buy an empty planet someplace for a dumping ground.

Every owner of a Two Acre Eden can do something about the garbage problem. He does not buy throwaway bottles, or nondegradable plastics if he can help it. Leaves, paper, grass clippings, and rags can all be composted — all are valuable as compost. I've even used old rugs as mulch with good results. Works perfectly. My wise, old English gardener neighbor (he's 90 and still does all his own work on his one-acre paradise) buries all his tin cans along his garden. He just keeps a trench going, about 18 inches deep, and fills and covers as needed. It takes years to get across his property, by which time, the tin he first buried is all rotted away. It's a very simple operation, really. Adds minerals to the soil, too.

Ecologists call such practices "self-containment." Each home recycles, and thereby consumes, its own wastes. No garbage problem, no pollution of streams. Nobody mentions it often, but a septic tank is a perfect example of self-containment. Septic tanks are a marvelous invention fallen into disrepute because half the time they aren't made right or because thoughtless people flush into them too many laundry detergents and other chemicals that slow down or destroy the bacterial action that makes a septic tank work. It is much easier to put sewers in all over the country at $2,000 per house, and flush all that crap out to the sewage disposal plant. Then, during heavy rains, the cities throw open the storm sewers and the swill goes rushing untreated into our rivers. This is progress?

In relation to the garden, specifically, I implement self-containment in a limited but practical manner in the following way. It starts with a small flock of hens.

For most people, keeping chickens poses an immediate problem. Ridiculous zoning laws prohibit many forms of livestock even on large lots. You can keep a blundering dog the size of a small elephant on a lot no bigger than a postage stamp, but you can't keep two hens on a half-acre. A lawyer friend of mine says this kind of zoning is probably unconstitutional. It ought to be. Any place large enough to keep a cat will serve for two hens without fuss or muss. And two hens can supply you with a dozen eggs a week.

Past this hurdle, here's how self-containment can work. You begin by raising corn for the chickens to eat.

The cornstalks are ranked around the coop in winter as insulation. In spring, they are ground up and used as bedding. Grass clippings from the lawn also become bedding. You can throw away the garbage disposal. The chickens eat all the table scraps and benefit from them, not to mention that you cut down on the amount of extra chicken feed you might have to buy. In the winter, we feed ours old lettuce that our groceryman would otherwise have to throw away. The chickens clean up most of the garden produce we don't eat. In the meantime, the chicks grow up and become broilers and fryers—meat that is high-quality, fresh, tasty. Unlike those who eat supermarket meat, we don't have to worry whether or not our chickens were really taken off that medicated feed formula ten days before they were butchered, as they were supposed to be. We know. Then pretty soon, the hens we don't butcher are producing eggs—the only way we've been able to get good eggs. Not only are fresh eggs better eating, but they make a vast difference in pastries and other food.

The chickens are also producing manure, mixing it into the litter, composting it into excellent fertilizer for the garden to make more food for more chickens for more eggs, and so on. You don't even have to make a compost pile. It's all very easy, improves the quality of your life, the richness of your soil, and adds nothing to pollution.

Many people tell me they'd like to use mulch on their garden but can't get enough. My advice: Subscribe to the *New York Times.* In even one year it should provide you enough mulch for a couple of acres. Seriously, newspapers do make good mulch. Spread a whole section —four or six pages thick—at a time and throw a clod or two on top so it won't blow away. I cover unsightly kinds of mulch like papers with leaves or grass clippings. I don't want my garden to look like a junk pile, even if that's what it really is. If you use newspapers for mulch, it's a good idea to add some nitrogen fertilizer to the ground where the newspapers are rotting.

If you use your fireplace a lot, or have wood-burning

stoves and furnaces, save the ashes and scatter them on your garden. Wood ashes contain lime and potash.

If you live out in the country, manure may be easier to get than you think. Most livestock farmers will be glad to give you some, if you do the hauling. In estate areas, where horses are popular, manure is a big problem, and you can generally find huge heaps of it rotting away behind the barns. Horse owners in such straits will welcome you and your pickup with open gates.

When I didn't have a truck, I traded garden produce with a friend for the use of his. The best find I've made is a horse farm where peat moss has been used as bedding, and a small mountain of peat moss and manure is composting away to beautiful richness.

On the other hand, if you happen to have a small farm near suburban areas, and have extra manure, you can sell it if you do the hauling. This may seem to contradict the preceding paragraph, but that is because human beings are so contradictory. The last time I bought a pickup load of manure ($8) the hauler told me he was able to sell all he had time to haul in the evenings. The first day he put an ad in the local paper, he had 16 calls from gardeners.

To get all the leaves we wanted, we found that it took only five persistent telephone calls to our local village street department to get a truckload delivered. Once the workers realized that our place was not as far to drive to as the nearest dump, they were only too glad to bring leaves. But the young fellow who drives the truck has grave doubts about our mental condition. "You just want me to dump them right here?" he always repeats in disbelief. "Yep." "All of them? Just dump them?" It is very difficult. The whole world cusses leaves in the fall. And we have all those trees around which to rake. And still we ask for more. He does not, will never, comprehend.

Grass clippings are my favorite mulch, even though (but also because) they rot down to nothing in a hurry. After I started mulching everything, I quickly realized that I needed a never-ending supply, which even my big lawn was incapable of giving me. So I began to approach people in the neighborhood who owned huge stretches of grass.

People are not used to having someone stop and ask them for their grass clippings. They don't believe you. They think you must be up to something nefarious, like maybe casing their home for a night burglary. There are several ways to overcome this problem. The best one is to use some other excuse for stoping by. If there are rumors of a new highway coming through your neighborhood, even if it is probably going to be ten miles away, you have the perfect entrée. It goes something like this:

"Hi." Me, waving. His mower is going full blast, and he doesn't really want to stop.

Silence, him. But he slacks off on the throttle and stops.

"Say, I live just down the road aways and . . ."

"Howsat?"

"I understand that someplace in this area there's A NEW ROAD COMING THROUGH."

He gets that all right and turns off the mower. There is a gleam in his eye that is just a mite dangerous.

"You say you're working on the new road?" he growls suspiciously.

"No, no." I know now which tack to take. "No, I'm just trying to figure out how to keep the damn thing out."

He relaxes, begins to polish his glasses. He is with a friend. Everybody in the whole world wants new highways to go someplace besides through or past their front door. Together we curse the government, the state, the highway department, the politicians, automobiles, population explosion, and every conniving local businessman who is working to get the highway close, but not too close, to his business. This easily takes a half hour, and with a little imagination, can chew up a whole afternoon of mulch-gardening. But finally the two of us are comrades who have fought the wars together. I turn to leave with a "Well, I just wondered if you knew any more about it than I did." When I get almost to the car, I let it occur to me, as if I had never thought of it before, to ask what he intended to do with all those grass clippings.

"Oh, I don't know. Dump 'em back over the hill, I guess."

"Say, I could use them. I grow a big garden and like to mulch around the plants."

"Be my guest," he says expansively. No one who opposes the highway could be all bad, even if he does queer things like collect grass clippings.

"Soon as you get them raked up, I'll be down," I say quickly. It is very important that you get started on the right track—having him and not you rake up the clippings. I zip off before he can reach the opposite conclusion.

I found a subdivision where the people are very, very particular about everything. The tradition, long established, is to fill plastic sacks with grass clippings and leave them for the garbage man to take. The garbage man comes on Monday morning, but I come on Saturday night, by prearrangement, and get at least a car trunk full. I could get a semi load, if I had one. Our car, as a result of these Saturday runs, smells like a silo all summer long.

Gathering grass clippings makes good neighbors eventually. It pleases them that they can please me and get rid of garbage at the same time. Even the garbage man is glad. And some of those clippings, from lawns fertilized so abundantly and at great cost, return the nutrients to my garden—shall I use a pun?—scot-free.

Chapter 7

The Most Unrottable
Compost Heap
I Ever Saw

"You don't make compost?" the gardener queried accusingly, in the same tone of voice my wife uses when asking, "You didn't take a bath?" I shuffled guiltily away from his mound of crumbly humus. It was obvious I could never enter the society of dedicated organic gardeners until I too could change garbage into fertile compost. It looked easy. All you did was pile a bunch of leaves or weeds or grass clippings with manure and any other decomposable, nitrogen-rich organic matter, and by and by it turned into an incomparable soil conditioner. Some organic gardeners were so adept at composting that I would not be surprised to learn that they could bury old refrigerators in their compost heaps and turn them into humus in six months.

Had not even so great a poet as Walt Whitman sung the joys of making compost? "Behold this compost! Behold it well!" he wrote in his usual effusive way. "It grows such sweet things out of such corruptions. . . . It gives such divine materials to men, and accepts such leavings from them at last." But such purple poetry sounds like mere droning compared to the lyrical tone of J. I. Rodale's *The Complete Book of Composting:*

> The composter watches over the heap like a hen with a newly hatched chick. He listens to its breathing and to its vaporous exhalations, feeling its pulse, taking its temperature twice a day and twelve times during the weekend. When he returns from work, he will run to it before kissing his wife. If it gives off an odor of ammonia, he knows he is losing nitrogen and will worry about it worse than if his child had the pox. . . . But the greatest pleasure of all is when our composter stands close to his heap in the gathering twilight, when the day's work is done. His whole being is filled with a sense of creation. He is mysteriously moved by the radiations and emanations of the heap. He is stirred by the thought that some vital force is at work which could improve the face of the earth, and he feels a part of and enveloped by a mighty God-force of creation.

If Job on his dunghill had only known, he would have been delighted with his lot. At least my spirit, no stranger to dunghills, was moved. I was not too keen on improving the face of the earth, but if feeling the pulse of a compost heap was more fun than kissing a wife, I wanted in on it.

I read every book on making compost I could find. On paper I knew how. But I had long ago discovered that knowing how on paper is not the same thing as knowing how from experience, so I looked up the neighborhood's most reputable compostmaker to see if he could turn old refrigerators into humus. So as not to appear a total ignoramus, I flashed my book of knowledge at him.

"Do you use the Indore method?" I asked primly.

"Oh no. I make all my compost outdoors," he replied.

I could see that this conversation was going to go nowhere fast. It appeared that Champion Composters just casually lumped together shredded leaves, grass clippings, table scraps, and a little dirt, and presto! three months later, having been shoveled from one mound to another, the aggregate turned into humus.

Anybody could do it, my reputable compostmaker allowed. Just to make sure, I hauled out the books again and religiously followed Sir Albert Howard's step-by-step procedure for making compost by his standard Indore method, a method that gardeners have used successfully all over the world. Whistling merrily with anticipation of partaking in "a mighty God-force of creation," I laid down a base of brush upon which to pile the organic materials that when changed into humus, would save the world. Next I spread a six-inch layer of leaves on the brush. Then a two-inch layer of manure from the henhouse and a two-inch layer of grass clippings over which I sprinkled a covering of topsoil and limestone with all the finesse of a gourmet cook adding spices to his roast. I repeated the layers until my heap stood about five feet tall and four feet square. I stood back and admired my handiwork. My being was filled with a sense of creation. I was moved by mysterious emanations and radiations. (I think it was the hen manure.) I slept the good sleep that night, certain that I had reversed the slide of modern civilization toward another Dark Age.

For six weeks I lingered in tense expectation at the foot of my beloved heap. I took its temperature, I felt its pulse, I listened for its vaporous exhalations. Nothing happened. I even tried not kissing my wife, but the only result of that maneuver was that she wanted to take *my* temperature. The heap remained nothing more than a heap. It did not heat, it did not exhale vaporously. It remained as inert and dead as a stone.

Undismayed, I "turned" it after 6 weeks like the book said and again after 12 weeks to allow air to penetrate all parts of the heap. Three months were soon up and the compost was supposed to be "finished." But all the heap contained were perfectly preserved leaves, hen manure, grass clippings, and soil. I could even see the whitish specks of the limestone. Only I was "finished."

I called in various Masters of Composting; one even

insisted that he had a Ph.D. in composting, since, as everyone knows, Ph.D. means "piled higher and deeper." The
Masters easily pointed out my error(s):

"Your heap is too dry. You should have added water
since it hasn't rained much."

"You can't really get good results unless you shred
and mix all your ingredients. Mere layering is too slow."

Why didn't somebody tell Sir Albert that? I went out
and bought a shredder, which helped save my garden
center proprietor, if not the world. Though it was now
August, I felt I could get another three months of activity
out of my heap once I shredded and moistened. I ground
up everything and mounded the batch into a neat pile
measuring four feet all around. By now I was at least
getting very good at making a neat pile. I could stack
the stuff up as plumb as a mason laying concrete blocks,
and top it off with a neat dome. I put a perforated pipe
down through the center of the heap for extra ventilation,
and as I built I moistened the ingredients by spraying
with a hose.

It took nearly two weeks of my spare time before
my imposing monument to a better world was completed.
The garden was weedy from neglect, and my wife com-
plained that I hardly ever kissed her anymore. She was
getting jealous of my mistress heap and muttered profanely
at it on her way to the henhouse to gather eggs.

I turned the heap in 6 weeks and wearily again in
12. The temperature of the thing was still not rising. Or
at least was not rising as fast as mine was. By the middle
of November, instead of dry leaves, clippings, and hen
manure, I had pickled leaves, clippings, and hen manure.
Compost it was not. Sweet smell it did not have. Its vaporous exhalations emanated sulfur.

I brought in more experts. They fussed, fumed,
stamped around, shook heads. Aha. An answer. I had used
tap water to moisten the heap. Very bad. Tap water has
too much chlorine in it, stupid. You must use rain water
or pure well water.

Oh boy. How about snow? The Masters all agreed

(more or less—when talking about compost heaps, the Masters almost always speak in conditional phrases) that winter is not a good time for decomposition in small heaps because the cold can penetrate into the heap too far. So I left the obstinate pile go and tried to plow under the weeds in the neglected garden. Perhaps the heap would weather away to humus over the winter. After all, even stones weather away in time.

Spring came and with it that irrational optimism that infects all gardeners. Never make a decision in early spring, but alas we all do. So complete was my irrationality that I not only decided to try once more to save the world with compost heaps, but this time I would use the famous "14-Day Composting Method" much heralded by *Organic Gardening* magazine, and first successfully perfected by the Sanitary Engineering Research Laboratory at the University of California at Berkeley. *The Complete Book of Composting* (Emmaus, Pennsylvania: Rodale, 13th printing, 1972), giving the historical background of the 14-day method, says that when the California engineers set out in 1949 to design a good method for composting municipal refuse, "they found a maze of conflicting claims in the semitechnical literature, but very few proven facts." I'll buy that. According to this method of making compost, the key is thorough grinding of the materials, which greatly increases the surface area on which microorganisms can multiply. Shredding finely also increases aeration, since shredded material doesn't pack down as much.

I ground up a new mess of herbage and manure, piled it in a handsome heap five feet tall, turned it just like the book said after three days, and then turned it every two or three days subsequently for two weeks.

Nothing happened except all the blisters broke on my heap-worn hands. Instead of the pile heating to a temperature of 140, it was my blood pressure that went to 140. I called the folks at *Organic Gardening*. Of the gardeners who really tried, 99 percent could make compost, so the problem was somehow me. Perhaps I didn't have faith enough. The nice fellow on the phone did not chuckle when I suggested that. No doubt he considered me some crackpot, and he was correct. But I got one morsel out of him that seemed helpful. He said that the process of composting can be greatly accelerated by adding some finished, or nearly finished, compost out of an old heap to the new heap.

So there it was. The perfect Catch-22. You couldn't make compost until you had some compost to make it with, and you couldn't get any compost to make it with until you made some compost.

I went begging around town for a bushel of the stuff, something I don't advise you to do if you are running for public office. Not enough people understand yet that in compost is the salvation of the world. The conversation will go something like this:

"Hi, Fred."

"Why are you carrying that bushel basket around, Logsdon? I don't have any tomatoes to give away."

"Oh, I just happened to have it with me. I was, ah, looking for something."

"Looking for something?" Fred was already suspicious, mistaking my hesitancy for evasiveness.

"Yea. Know anybody in our neighborhood who makes compost?"

"Makes compost?"

"Oh, you know. You make it out of piles of rotten leaves and stuff like that."

"Who would want to make it with a rotten leaf?" He thought that was very funny. He said to try old Wilbur Jones across the street.

Old Wilbur thought he had been approached for every kind of crazy contribution to society a mad world could devise, but this was the first time anyone had ever asked him for compost. He eyed me suspiciously. "You from the health department? You wanna get a sample of my compost to see if it's got germs in it, don't you? Somebody's been complainin' about my compost, ain't they? Look, how many times I gotta prove to you people compost don't stink, don't shelter rats, don't make flies? Go away."

Finally, almost on bended knees, I won his trust. He let me have a bushel of compost. Just as I was leaving, a thought occurred to me. "Say, when you made your first compost heap, did you borrow some compost to start it with?"

He thought on it. "That's been a long time ago, son. Let's see. Did I get some from Uncle Eb? No, he got his'n from me. And the boys got theirs from him. Hmmmm." He scratched his head. Compost was like sourdough. You had to get a starter from somewhere else, it seemed. Only God knows where the first sourdough and compost came from. Probably Adam and Eve. "Nope," I didn't have to borrow any," Wilbur finally concluded. "Just made my own."

"How long did it take to turn your first compost heap into humus? I asked.

"Oh, I pile 'em up and just leave 'em sit for a few years."

"A few *years*?"

"Sure. Rome wasn't built in a day."

You can see why I have become an ardent sheet composter. I hope you will forgive me, Sir Albert, but it works out better for a man of little faith, to spread his compostable materials out into a six-inch layer over the garden and let them rot to humus in nature's own time and manner. I know I'm not getting the best benefits from the mulch that way, but it's either that or the end of matrimonial bliss. My wife will not play second fiddle to a dunghill.

Sheet composting has its own merits for the busy gardener like me who puts out more garden than he needs. As mulch, the compostable leaves and grass clippings and chicken bedding smother out weeds and preserve moisture. Mulch draws the worms up to the soil surface to work their wonders of fertility and in the process aerate the soil. And once in place, mulch requires no more labor than perhaps pulling it back temporarily in the spring so the ground underneath warms up faster. Properly managed, mulch will not even require this operation, since in a normally humid climate most of the preceding year's application will have rotted away by spring.

There is something to be said, too, about having the

actual process of humic decay occurring on the soil surface. I have observed this decaying process too often to doubt anymore; there is something *extra* in the way of fertility happening when organic matter is actually decaying in contact with the soil. There is an energy there beyond both the soil's and the mulch's measurable content of nutrients that makes plants grow better. I have seen plants on the poorest clay subsoils spark to vigorous growth with no other help than a layer of decaying mulch. Take the decaying mulch away and the plants immediately begin to lose their vitality. Nor will the plants grow as well in the mulch only. There is something happening right there on that thin line between mulch and soil; no doubt, those same mysterious emanations and radiations Sir Albert divined coming from his compost heap.

There's really only one point on which I disagree in principle with the proponents of compost heaps. Compost could indeed make a better world, heaped or sheeted, but it will never take the place of kissing your wife.

Chapter 8

If You Mean Rabbits,
Praise Ecology
But Pass the Ammunition

I'm forever amazed when reading gardening periodicals and books at the way the main problem is glossed over when it comes to raising backyard food. Horticultural energy seems to be expended arguing about how much of Ortho's latest I should or should not drench my vegetables with, or whether mulch will cover weeds or just a multitude of sins, or how rotary tillers will do everything except pick apples. But it's not the bugs, blights, and weeds that do me in. It's the damned birds and beasts. If Sir Albert Howard had spent more time learning how to compost rabbits instead of manure, we'd be able to raise all the food in our backyards that we need, with enough left over to help India out of a famine or two.

Who has yet found a reliable way to keep robins from eating cherries? Coons out of ripe sweet corn? Moles out of lawns? Chipmunks out of strawberries? A whole host of feathered friends out of sprouting corn? Or ripe blueberries? After 30 years behind the hoe, I have collected a list of animal and bird control methods, which I have categorized in the "do work" column and the "do not work" column. The "do not" column is as long as your arm; the "do" column I can sum up in two words: proper fencing.

The myths I'll talk about first, since when gardening manuals do get around to the subject of varmints the myths are what they delude us with. As far as I can find out from others, and certainly in all my own experience, there is no scare device made that will fool a bird or animal very long. Scarecrows, plastic owls, snakelike hoses entwined in the trees, shining strips of metal, aluminum disks swaying in the breeze, cross-hatches of string strung above the plants, windmills, whirligigs, wind chimes, explosives, recorded sounds of alarm in bird language, recordings of cursing farmers—none of these work. Not long enough. Once two divinity students got into an argument about predestination and free will while visiting me. I positioned them under a fruiting cherry tree, and the robins flew away for only ten minutes. As far as I can tell, when a robin gets a ripe cherry in its sights, it will fly right through a cat's whiskers to get it.

That is not quite true. In the interest of science, I must qualify that statement—and this is true. A robin doesn't eat so many *ripe* cherries. He eats them all before they get ripe. If your tree is larger than the local robin population, you may, at the end of the season, get a pie or two of very nice ripe cherries. The robins, I reason, finally get too sick from green cherries to polish off the entire crop.

Secondly, there is no scent noxious enough to scare away hungry animals for very long. Blood, urine, blood meal, dead animal carcasses, used oil, gasoline, kerosene, mothballs, chili powder, or any commercial concoction of the fakelore folk remedies are not effective for any length of time. I used to be afraid to say that in writing because there is always the possibility that my stray dogs, cats, birds, deer, coons, groundhogs, chipmunks, squirrels, rabbits, and shrews are smarter or have less delicate noses than varmints in other parts of the country. But now I have scientific support for my statement. The University of Illinois took the time to test a wide sampling of traditional and commercial rabbit repellents, including that old standby, chili powder. They applied the repellents to cabbage plants in three replications each, including an untreated row to compare against. The cabbages were enclosed in fencing and rabbits put inside. The cussed creatures ate *every* cabbage plant, just like I knew they would, even though they were being fed their customary ration of rabbit pellets. In other words, they weren't even all that hungry. One of the researchers says he thought the rabbits particularly relished the cabbages coated with chili powder.

Of course, there are flaws in this test, the kind of flaws that keep the folk beliefs alive, right or wrong. Rabbits being fed pellets in an enclosed area are probably hungrier for a change in diet than wild rabbits nibbling away at 100 different kinds of wild plants. So the former ones might be more inclined to chew right through chili powder or even creosote. Nevertheless, the evidence still suggests strongly that there is no practical repellent discovered yet that will stop a hungry rabbit for long — and in early spring after a long lean winter, there is nothing hungrier than a rabbit.

Just to show you how vainglorious are any attempts to scare animals away from your luscious fruits and vegetables, I want to tell you about an acquaintance of mine who has pursued these methods longer than I have, using all the craftiness and technology available. Sly Engineer (not his real name) lives in southern Ohio where coons will soon outnumber people if gardeners persist in growing sweet corn for them every year. Sly reviewed the calculations in his little black gardening notebook one August (engineers are forever writing figures in notebooks), and noted that 95 percent of his sweet corn was being eaten by raccoons. Engineers, especially when they garden, do not like that kind of arithmetic. So old Sly set a lighted lantern in his corn patch and congratulated himself on saving electricity. The coons had never seen a lantern before, but it took their counterintelligence agents less than three days to determine that the thing was harmless unless swallowed.

Sly got about 6 ears of corn close to the lantern, and the coons got 66 farther away. Sly replaced the lantern with an electric light that winked on and off; to hell with saving kilowatts. The coons winked right back after the third night of this nonsense and went on munching corn.

Sly Engineer, used to solving problems of great magnitude, began to do a slow burn. All winter he consulted the oracles of scientific fact and unscientific tradition. By late the next summer he was ready. No coon was going to outwit *Homo sapiens,* especially *Homo sapiens* var. *Engineer.*

First he strung creosote-soaked twine 18 inches off the ground in all directions. Sly actually enjoyed a few meals of corn before the coons wised up.

Sly was wising up too, but he didn't know it yet. Had one wandered past his corn patch in the following weeks, one would have thought Sly had rented his garden to a carnival. Lights now winked inside yellow plastic buckets. Between winks, doorbells attached to batteries and a timer rang from the cornstalks. I am *not* kidding. Along with the noise, the heavy aroma of creosote dripping from 1,000 strings clung heavily to the night air. It was a ghastly marvel of electronic gadgetry and gas warfare. It confused the coons hardly more than five nights as they waited for the next planting of corn to ripen up.

Sly applied electronic warfare to his fruit trees when birds attacked too. But he tried humbler methods first. He hung tin cans in cherry trees in an ingenious manner only an engineer could think up. He hung the cans upside down, each by a wire inserted through a hole in the bottom. The wire was bent into a sort of hook so the can couldn't slip off. As the can swayed (hopefully) in the breeze, the wire hook scraped against the inside wall of the can giving rise to a noise that was supposed to paralyze robins with fear. When the sound of musical cans turned to dinner music to the birds, Sly started setting off firecrackers and shooting shotguns into the air. The crows went away, but all the rest of the birds gaily pecking holes in apples and peaches seemed totally unimpressed. He tried the old flashing-light routine. No go. In desperation, he hung a radio in his favorite tree and tuned it to the most powerful local station. The birds loved it.

But then, eureka. Sly turned to a rock station—the kind of noise only a deaf teenager can endure—and turned up the volume. For three days. The birds went away and never came back, Sly claims. Had he played that noise a fourth day, his neighbors would have gone away and never come back either.

I have tried mothballs in the garden to fend off coons. One year, I got so angry, I took a sackful of mothball crystals and flung them madly around the patch. The depredations stopped for a few nights. The garden smelled like a formal black-tie-and-cummerbund dinner party. But we were able to get enough corn to freeze some before the coons came back. Unfortunately, in my rage, I had overdone it and some of those crystals had lodged in the crotches between the corn ears and stalks. Believe it or not, the odor so persisted that even when we ate the frozen corn, we could taste mothballs. And that's the solemn truth.

The underground attackers, moles and pocket gophers, are even harder to deal with. You can trap them. You can poison them. Neither method is too effective. Moles are far less harmful than most people think. They will ruin the looks of a lawn, but even when they tunnel down your garden rows, they don't usually hurt the vegetables too much. They eat worms mostly. Pocket gophers are something else. I trapped them in Minnesota where I once had a garden, but it seemed that for every one I caught, two more came to dig holes.

The cage traps that catch animals alive and unharmed are best for aboveground animals in the garden, but the traps won't really solve the problem unless you are very persistent and skillful. The Havahart people probably won't believe me, but their standard trap won't catch squirrels, though it works fine for other animals. A squirrel is too fast. It can enter the cage, trip the trap, but scoot back out before the doors at either end fall closed. We've watched them do it. No matter how finely I set the trap's trigger, the squirrels win. Even when you see it, you can't believe it.

Use of live traps has resulted in what I consider a detestable practice on the part of urban gardeners. They will catch a wild pest animal and then, exuding great kindness for wildlife, transport it out to the country areas, like where I live, and free it. They do the same with cats and dogs that they have been irresponsible enough to allow to come into existence. Setting wild animals free in a new territory displays a particularly narrow knowledge of ecology. Our common native animals occupy the land fully wherever food and habitat are suitable. Bringing in a stranger helps nothing. The natives will drive it out by territorial imperative, or it will starve, or it will upset the delicate balance already established there. And you will definitely upset the balance of peace and understanding established between country and adjacent urban residents.

After you have tried all the fakelore and vented 10,000 curse words on its failure, you will decide that the only reliable way to protect a garden against birds and animals is with proper fencing or screening. Sometimes fencing is easy; most often it is difficult and requires a serious investment of time and money. But once done, a good fence will last a long time and make your gardening so much more pleasant, you will never regret the work you put into it.

Rabbits, thank heavens, are fairly easy to fence out. Chicken wire two feet tall is all you need. You don't even have to install it super tight and super strong as you would most fences. So long as the fencing is fairly tight and reaches to the soil level, it will keep out rabbits. They do not try very much to scoot or dig under the fence and they can't climb over it. Light stakes pounded into the ground every four feet will hold the fence up adequately, with somewhat heavier stakes at the corners. Pieces of two by four driven a foot into the ground are adequate for corner posts, one-by-three furring for other posts. A rabbit fence can be moved to different areas of the garden fairly easily. If you use the small steel or fiberglass electric fence stakes, which you can push and pull in and out of the ground easily, the job of fencing a pea patch won't be difficult.

All varmints that can climb a fence, have to be controlled with electric fence. Some gardeners use only a single strand about six inches off the ground to control coons and groundhogs, but two strands, the second another six inches above the first, are more effective. You have to keep weeds from shorting out the line. Use steel posts as coons will sometimes figure out a way to climb wooden posts without touching the wire. The objection I have to steel posts is that sometimes songbirds will land on the fence with one foot on the wire and the other on the post. That grounds them and electrocutes them. Two solutions: Use the low-voltage systems out now that give a small shock adequate enough to deter small animals, rather than a conventional charger which can rock a horse back on its haunches; or use the new fiberglass posts, which are nonconductive.

In deer country, gardeners say electric fencing won't work. Deer jump over or get entangled and break the fence. But researchers at Penn State University have designed an electric fence they claim is deerproof.

Since groundhogs are burrowers, some gardeners fear they will dig under a fence. They might, but generally they do their digging only at their den sites. If they decide to dig a den in your garden, you can discourage them by digging their holes open about two feet and jamming the excavation with rocks and dirt. I've done this often. The groundhogs promptly go someplace else to dig their dens. It is hard work, but actually takes less time than fiddling around with smoke or gas bombs or other concoctions. I've often watched, but never yet have seen a groundhog forced out of its hole by smoke.

Chipmunks are not always bothersome, but they will take a whole bush full of gooseberries or a small patch of strawberries in no time at all if they get the notion. A one-inch wire-mesh fence completely around and over a plant is necessary, or a low fence with strands of electric fence at the bottom and at the top. Squirrels are a terrible problem in nut groves, of course, but seldom in the garden. They can develop a keen taste for black raspberries, however. A fence like the chipmunk arrangement will work, though the mesh size need not be as small. In nut groves, guns, traps, and trained dogs help. If you have an English walnut grove in a town where English walnuts are unusual, you may have to do what one such grower did—invest a lot of money in a chain link fence. A chain link fence does fairly well in keeping out those smartest of all varmints, small children.

Where birds eat your fruit, the only defense is a strong screen completely around and over the plants. That means first of all that the plants have to be relatively small, hardly more than six feet or so tall. Blueberries and dwarf fruit trees fit this category. There are even some new natural dwarf varieties of cherries and sweet cherries coming on the market—probably the only practical cherries for bird lovers' backyards.

Wire mesh is always better than a fabric netting, but if you use the latter, you cannot just drape it over the tree or bush the way those charming advertising pictures show. Draping the netting might save a few fruits at the center of the tree, but the birds will land on the netting and peck right through the netting into the fruit on the outside (where most of the fruit grows). If you must drape, cheesecloth is better than wide-mesh fabric or plastic netting. Cheesecloth works fairly well on strawberries.

But particularly for blueberries, which I think are birddom's favorite dish, a permanent screen fence around and over the bushes is the only answer. Set stout, rot-resistant posts down both sides of the row or rows of bushes with two-by-four stretchers connecting all the posts at the top. Nail fine-mesh wire fencing around the posts and drape a roof of the same over the stretchers. Nail or wire it down tightly, too. A screen door makes a bird-tight entrance.

It is even better to make up four-foot by eight-foot

panels of wire mesh framed by one-by-four boards. Then instead of nailing and wiring the mesh to the posts and over the stretchers, you set up the panels and bolt them or affix them in some other way to the posts and stretchers. These panels can then be taken down after the fruiting season and be stored inside. They should last as long as you live and, except during the fruiting season, you can work around your bushes without being hampered for space by the screening. Four bushes of blueberries so protected will produce more fruit for *you* than a dozen unprotected bushes.

The other universal problem among gardeners is how to keep birds from eating newly sprouted seeds, particularly corn. You can't shoot your way out of this problem, tempting as it may seem. There are three or four partially effective defenses, which when used in combination, will save enough corn to keep the coons from going hungry in August.

1. Resist the temptation to plant extra early corn. It's that first corn the birds like to eat the best, just like us. Instead, try to plant your first corn when the heaviest local planting is taking place. In a farming community, plant when (or a day after) most farmers are planting theirs. In a town, tell your neighbors you are going to plant corn, but don't. They will all rush out and plant theirs so you don't get ahead of them. Plant a day after they do, and the birds may fill up on their sprouting corn and forget yours. Remember, the birds go after the corn for only about four days—when the corn is just coming up. If you could get the whole town to plant corn on the same day, the birds would only get a percentage of the crop. But staggered plantings from one neighborhood to the next make it easy for them to flock from garden to garden and clean everyone out.

2. You can coat seeds with a mixture of tar and gasoline. It won't hurt the seed. This seems to slow down, but not stop, the bird depredations.

3. I have in the last two years, planted oats with the corn. The oats sprout first. The birds don't like oat sprouts and so far, knock on wood, they don't seem to

notice the corn nudging through the ground behind the oats. Later, I weed out the oats in the interest of neatness. I don't think a little oats in the row hurts anything, though.

4. In the last four years I have spread an inch of chicken manure compost over the planted corn. This practice also seems to deter the birds, in addition to giving a wonderful boost to the corn.

All this makes corn planting a complicated job, but it's worth it. Actually, I have quit the tar and gasoline routine because it makes the seed too gooey to plant with my little hand-pushed seeder. And I'm not sure which of the other three measures is the key to my newfound success in saving sprouting corn. I'm afraid to grow corn using only one of the combination for fear the birds will get it all.

In any event, be very slow to kill any varmint. I'm kind of a hypocrite to say that, since I've killed my share of rabbits and groundhogs. But even a blasted rabbit does some good — as an occasional meal for beneficial hawks and owls. There's so much we don't know and find out only painfully. One year I noticed a lot of redwing blackbirds patrolling my corn patch and assumed they were eating the sprouting corn. I suppose they did eat some. I shot a few. Later I read that redwings are great eaters of cutworms. I started watching the birds with binoculars. Sure enough, they were walking up and down the rows not touching the corn at all, but eating bugs and worms. I might add that we have many redwings, but never problems with cutworms, though such problems are very common in this region. Far better to lose some corn to birds than to an infestation of cutworms.

Chapter 9

You Can Do More about the Weather than the Weather Bureau Can

I think the weather bureau has sold its soul to some conniving bunch of public relations experts. Or perhaps it has learned a lesson from the ancient Greek oracles: Say nothing, but use a lot of high-toned words to make nothing sound clever. A typical weather report lasts 5 minutes squeezed between seven commercials, during 4½ minutes of which the weatherman elaborates on the present and past weather, which we know already, then spends maybe 30 seconds telling us what might happen tomorrow but rarely does. If you are a gardener depending on a weather report, you can get a more accurate picture by watching a televised ball game from an area about 200 miles west of you, unless you live in California. If it's raining at the ball game, it will no doubt be raining at your place the next day; if fair there, it will probably be fair at your place the next day. At least the odds are something like 60 to 40 to that effect, which is all the better the weather bureau can do. Only they spend millions of tax dollars doing it.

Weather forecasting did not quite reach its zenith

of pathos and grandeur until 1973, when some wild meteo-
rologist, infected with the doomsday psychology of the
times, looked into his crystal spectrum-spanner and perceived that glaciers had been sighted above Nome, Alaska,
possibly moving toward Detroit at the speed of 1¾ feet per
decade. My God. In a few short eons we might all have to
flee to Equador or freeze to death. The ice age cometh
again. Corn will stop growing. Peaches will mold on the
trees. Bikinis will mildew in the closet.

Alas for the weather "mumbo-jumblers," the winters
of 1973/74, 1974/75, and 1975/76 were as mild as warm
milk. The fuel "mumbo-jumblers" told us the only reason
there was not a fuel shortage was the unusually mild
weather, though I don't believe them any more than I
believe the weather bureau.

This turn of events should have embarrassed the
fake forecasters, but the more nimble among them simply
slid over to the other end of the weather spectrum and
began telling us in the fall of '76, about the "greenhouse
effect" which was warming up the atmosphere. The greenhouse effect, they said, resulted from polluted air hanging
like a pall over the earth, holding in the heat reflected
from the sun. At the present rate of warming, earth would
turn into an inferno in only 45 billion years.

These knowing predictions were followed by the
winter of 1976/77, the coldest in our history, which was
followed by the winter of 1977/78, nearly as cold and
with much more snow.

The weather soothsayers love it. They can't lose. If
the temperature falls to record lows, they point fearfully
at the glaciers and go cash their ill-gotten paychecks. If
the temperature soars to record highs, they expound on
carbon dioxide and the greenhouse effect all the way to
the bank. They study the entrails of their statistics. They
pound to powder their triplicate forms and boil them in
the cauldrons of their computers. They listen to the divina-
tions and incantations of the bureaucratic process; they
consort with the vampires of federal grants. They know we
don't care what they predict, so long as it is not too soothing.

Two Acre Eden

We pay them to keep us from worrying about something that needs worrying about—like our sanity. Already they have' new theories lurking in the wings of the six o'clock news, just in case the glaciers start to melt and the air pollution begins to dissipate. There is always the possibility that a slight shift in the gravitational-magnetic fields of interplanetary space might lurch the earth from its normal course through the heavens 1/2,000th of a meter closer to the sun. We would then soon burn up in a matter of only 3 billion years. Expect average temperatures next summer of 112 degrees F. unless we switch to the metric system. The rivers will run dry; the seas will shrink. There will be no beer, even in Milwaukee—a sobering thought. Of course if we lurch 1/2,000th of a meter *away* from the sun, then we will *freeze* to death within a short 3 billion years, glacier or no glacier. The Greek oracles would have been green with envy at such a marvelous racket.

There is a way to protect ourselves from this lunacy. Fight fire with fire, I say, or perhaps ice with ice. If so-called scientists are going to run around like religious crackpots predicting the end of the world, then we must counter with our own folklore. It has a much better track record. We shall see whose medicine is stronger.

Potatoes planted in the dark of the moon will grow, ice age coming or not. Have your grain planted by a nude, pregnant woman during full moon when the sign of the zodiac rests in the arms going down to the bowels, and you will have a bumper crop, even in polluted air. The ancient Goths knew how to handle glaciers and such. Cut the heart out of an evergreen tree and burn it in your fireplace on the shortest day of the year and there's a 100 percent chance that spring will come again in its proper season. It works every time. To stop a glacier, hang mistletoe over your door frame. They've been doing it in Kentucky for centuries and approaching glaciers never reach beyond the Ohio River before receding again.

In a slightly more serious vein, folklore *can* help you predict the weather at least as well as the National Weather Service can. "Red sky at night, sailor's delight; red sky in the morning, sailor's warning" is a surer bet than when some long-lashed femme fatale who has never seen a sunset murmurs sexily over the radio that there's a 50 percent chance of fair weather tomorrow. Smoke laying low to the ground instead of rising promptly into the air is a sure sign of rain, unless you are in Jersey City. When the sound of trains carries far into the night air, it usually rains. A circle around the moon portends a better than 50 percent chance of rain within three days. Sun dogs, or mock suns that appear as bright spots on one or both sides of the evening sun are almost always heralds of stormy weather. If your rheumatiz flares up, or an old scar prickles, look for rain. Static on an AM radio means rain or a broken aerial. Ants scurrying in panic over an anthill for no apparent reason often tell you a quick summer storm is going to strike. A heavy dew means clear weather the day following. A dense fog in the morning brings a sunny afternoon. "Rain before 7, won't stop till 11." Whirlwinds bring rain, especially whirlwinds that move toward the sun, but the rain may be a few days in coming. Mare's tails clouds mean windy weather. Mackerel skies are a sign of unsettled weather. When skies clear toward evening after early spring rain, with a wind continuing from the northwest fairly strong and growing colder, expect dying winds and frost after midnight. East winds never bring any good— either too much rain or snow. All signs fail in dry weather. When a hog scratches its back, look for rain. If the sun shines while rain falls, rain will fall again tomorrow. Heavy coats of winter hair on animals mean a colder than usual winter. When flies bite hard, look for rain. When you hear the first katydid in August, frost is six weeks away. When the bluebirds come back, spring has come for sure, and there will be no more cold weather. If the groundhog sees his shadow on February 2, there'll be six more weeks of cold weather. Plant corn when oak leaves are as big as squirrel ears. If you want it to rain, wash the car or cut some hay.

All those folk beliefs may not be correct, but I guarantee them to out-predict any weather report on TV and the *Old Farmer's Almanac* to boot.

There is a more general kind of weather predicting you really can do if you keep close records of your local weather and its effect on your garden. You need to keep such records or a garden diary for at least five years, but a ten-year record is better. Studying your diary is more help than you might at first realize in pinpointing almost to the day, or at least within several days, when you will be needed in the garden and for what purpose. Since we all garden in our spare time; or work our homesteading around a full-time job, it's very handy to know when we'll be free to travel, to vacation, to accept an overnight invitation, or when we *must* be at home to attend to food production. If you keep garden diaries, you know how amazingly regular your planting and harvest dates are, despite late springs, early winters, and cool summers. Strawberries get ripe nearly the same time every year — '78 is the only real exception in my records — when the berries ripened a week late. I know that come hell or high water, I will be planting the first garden sometime in the last week of April. I plant the biggest share of the corn around May 9, set out frost-tender plants on May 20, plant lima beans on May 25. There is a rhythm to the seasons that does not hear the dire soothsayers of the National Weather Service.

Your records may pinpoint crucial periods of time different from those of other gardeners, even in your own neighborhood. A nearby market gardener friend of mine has a much sandier soil than my clay. He is generally a good two weeks ahead of me in the spring, because his ground warms up faster and drains better. He is also next to a body of water large enough to influence frost severity a little from what we must content with just three miles away. His records wouldn't help me very much.

To help you keep better track of the weather, you need a rain gauge and a minimum-maximum thermometer. You get enough fun out of both of them to warrant the purchase — you can whoop at the weather bureau when they predict a low of 28 ruining your apple blossoms, and you get up in the morning and find, on your thermometer, the low was only 33.

Gardeners always like to know how much rain they're getting, and the knowledge can be handy, too. I remember one year when things looked peaked in the orchard even though we had seemed to have enjoyed a goodly number of rainy days. I checked with a gardener who had a rain gauge, and sure enough, we had had plenty of rainy *days* but like politicians, those days were mostly bluster and little substance. The amount of rain that had fallen was small and if I didn't get out there and put the hose to that new tree, it wasn't going to make the grade. I bought a rain gauge.

In rural areas, you can get the soil temperature reading every day in the spring from the radio if you listen to programs directed toward the farm audience. But since your garden may warm up sooner or later than the norm for your region, you can use a soil thermometer of your own. A soil moisture meter is also handy, especially for indoor plants, hotbeds, and cold frames. Until your top layers of soil warm up to at least 60 degrees F., planting a garden is just asking for trouble in my experience.

You won't use a wind gauge a whole lot, but if you like keeping weather records, you can amaze your friends by casually pointing out that your tree blew down even though the weatherman reported only 25 mile per hour winds, because actually the wind was gusting to 45 mph around your house. The value of a wind gauge is to focus your attention on the effect of wind on gardening. Wind wrecks flowers; bends little trees to a 45-degree angle; breaks over raspberry canes, corn, cane sorghum, laden branches of fruit, grapevines (even when tied — but not securely enough), tender young tomato plants, oat and wheat stalks heavy with grain. Winter winds sear evergreens, pile snowdrifts around young fruit trees, which then break down under the weight of the snow when it melts. In short, wind is a grave nuisance to gardening. Checking your wind gauge will persuade you to get those new trees staked; plant gardens in protected spots on the lee side of house, garage, or woodlot; and plant shade trees and windbreaks wherever you can. With shade trees hovering around your house, you create your own check against those "record highs" the weather bureau reports in July. With a good windbreak, your windchill factor will never be as bad as the weatherman says. And tender plants and shallow-rooted dwarf trees will survive better behind it.

There are other ways to make your own weather, so to speak. You know what a crimp rain on your day off can put into your gardening plans, to say nothing of golfing plans. But it is possible to carry on normal garden work in the rain or at least in spite of rain, *if* you follow a serious mulching method that upgrades your soil with a high content of organic matter. What happens is that soil can become so spongy with good humusy tilth that it simply doesn't get muddy enough from rain to halt shallow cultivation, hoeing, and hand-pulling weeds. Sandy soil to which large yearly applications of organic matter have been made can reach this kind of texture much sooner than clayey soils, but in time, the latter also will mellow.

Many organic gardeners told me this kind of tilth could be achieved on clay, but I had to do it myself before I believed them. I heaped leaves and manure and grass clippings and shredded tree bark and straw on one of my gardens for five years—about a foot deep each year. The clay earth underneath was rarely disturbed except where I would dig out a hole to set vegetable transplants in. Gradually the mulches broke down into crumbly, soil-like humus. This humus is now about six inches deep, and I can cultivate it with my shoe, or more often, my toes, ruffling the surface to destroy germinating weeds and making shallow planting trenches for dropping in seeds—even on rainy days or at most after only a couple hours of drying time. It is even possible to cultivate that soon after rain with the tiller, but only shallowly. My planting methods in this humus are extremely careless and casual, but nearly everything grows. I think broomsticks would sprout there. Most of the "weeds" that come up are volunteer vegetables from the leftovers of last year's crop. In another ten years of mulch care and what I call "slop-gardening," I probably won't have to plant anything at all. The garden will simply renew itself in an annual vegetable jungle.

This kind of mulch-gardening is also the best cure for lack of rain. Even in dry years, the soil under a good mulch remains reasonably moist. Instead of cussing the weatherman when the summer showers he predicts don't come, you can sit back and bless your mulch.

Where climates are very dry and some irrigation is necessary, you will find a combination of mulching and drip irrigation will make a liar out of weather reports that warn of drought. Drip irrigation and mulching are easy on your pocketbook and on dwindling water supplies. Running a drip hose under mulch saves every drop of water for the plants, whereas sprinkling allows much of the water to evaporate. Drip-irrigation systems are sold by all good nursery centers.

You can also extend your growing season beyond what the weather bureau measures for your area. I have mixed feelings about how much time a homesteader or gardener ought to spend tinkering with structures that provide artifical growing atmospheres for plants (the time might be better spent canning and preserving). But if not some kind of greenhouse, at least hotbeds and cold frames and indoor starting beds under special growing bulbs may be worthwhile sometimes, especially in an area with a very short natural growing season. I've decreased my use of artificial structures, but I still find a hotbed handy in the spring and a cold frame in the fall. I grow early lettuce in the spring, plus some plants to set out, and both lettuce and spinach for salads in the fall, up until about Thanksgiving. For frames I simply nail together some old pieces of two by tens, scrounged from a dilapidated barn, into a boxlike frame about six feet square, set it on the ground, dig out the soil about two feet deep and pile it around the outside of the boards, put a foot of heating horse manure in the bottom of the hole and about a foot of topsoil on top of that, plant, and cover the frame with a piece of clear plastic. In late summer, with the first crop long gone, I spade up the soil in the bed a little, smooth, and plant. When days get cold, I put the plastic cover back on when necessary. I've grown watercress for a late crop, which requires almost daily watering. Oak leaf lettuce and Long Standing Bloomsdale spinach seem to be the best for cold endurance.

If you go to more elaborate solar greenhouse structures, I will cheer for you but not follow. At least not yet. I am busy enough cheating the frost out of food in my wintry gardens to spend the time (and money) on greenhouses, though I dearly want to try someday. Until then, I have kale and endive right from the garden until mid-November. One year I curled a plastic panel for frost protection over an eight-foot-long endive row, and we managed to pick enough for a salad on Christmas. Tomatoes wrapped and stored last till November 15, indoors. Potatoes last all winter, and so do onions, which I store in barrels buried to the brim in the yard. Carrots, under piles of leaves in the garden last until March. Parsnips are ready to eat in March also. We have found that late watermelons will sometimes continue to ripen even after light frost has killed the leaves but not the vines. Such watermelons can lay right out in the garden until the middle of November and still be worth eating. Our winter nest onions — perennials — are ready to eat almost as quickly as the snow recedes in March. There's maple syrup to gather in March; the stored grains to grind for flour all winter; squash on the cellar shelves still good in January; persimmons and late apples still on the trees in November, not to mention hickory nuts (see chapter 19, "How to Beat Winter"). In other words, I can eat well without a greenhouse but intend to get one as soon as someone invents a 30-hour day.

You can protect fruits from frost too, though I sometimes wonder if it pays. In the spring of '79, the weather report waved a red flag of "Frost Alert" at us four times during apple and strawberry blossom time, and the report was wrong every time. Then one night when the temperature was supposed to go only to 35, it went to 29. Back-yarders who had four times thrown blankets over dwarf trees didn't that night, and so the weatherman took as awful a beating as the trees.

I have ceased to worry about frost. What will be, will be. I've planted late apples and early apples, late berries and early berries, and I've never seen frost get them all . . . well, only once. I try to keep both tree and bush fruits dormant as long as I can with mulch that keeps the ground from thawing out early, but after that, it is, as they say, in the hands of the Lord. I've gone through that act of trying to keep smudge pots smoking, or trying to dress a fruit tree in an old blanket, even trying to raise night-time temperature by sprinkling water over berries. I just don't think any of that pays unless you are a commercial grower equipped to make it pay. We have just as many apples, cherries, pears, strawberries, raspberries, blue-berries, elderberries, and melons now that I don't worry about frost as we did when I did worry about it. Let the weatherman worry—he gets paid for it.

Chapter 10

In Backyard
Food Production,
Timing Is Everything

Baseball players aren't the only people who have trouble with their timing. Gardeners do too. In fact, poor timing is the main problem with novice and sometimes not so novice gardeners. And when your timing is off in gardening, everything is chaos and misery.

It happens to be a June 15 as I write this and I have just driven my son six miles to a farm where he helps make hay. Going and coming I passed many gardens, some models of skill and economy (in the original meaning of that word) but most, I am sorry to say, were rather forlorn. I'll describe one of these homesteads in detail because I know something of the background to it, and you'll see what I mean. Jack Procrastinator and his wife Judy, whose maiden name was Tardy, moved out into the country three years ago to live a more independent life. The farmer who was supposed to plow their garden for them (an Uncle Tardy) didn't get to it until the middle of May, and the Procrastinators in three years haven't caught up yet. They are eager, willing to learn, mean well, and are really very likeable folks, but they do not understand that time and nature wait on no man and very few women. They work hard at home and in their factory jobs, but think a food production system can be shut down like an assembly line when the workday is over. They haven't realized yet that if you really want to be at least partially food independent, fuel independent, and power independent, it takes a full-time commitment in relation to which all other activities, including sleeping and playing, must take a backseat sometimes.

Everything is at loose ends with the Procrastinators. The tiller is broken and Jack is trying to fix it while the weeds grow, the corn turns yellow, and the soil, worked when it was too wet in the first place, bakes to cement in the sun. His bees are swarming because he didn't get another super on the hive in time. A dry nanny goat, knee-deep in manure, bleats hungrily from a small shed. She could at least be eating the weeds in her lot, but the fence needs mending before she can be let out. Five ancient hens, none of them laying, wander in the yard, leaving droppings on the unfinished sidewalk. The Procrastinators do not mind the manure on the sidewalk—they think that makes them more genuinely "farmy"—although farmers I know would be mortified. Judy tries to hoe the corn, but the hoe bounces off the clods as if off wood. She pulls weeds by hand but soon wearies because of the shear number of them. Those weeds could easily have been demolished if attacked when they were just germinating. It's too late now.

The whole place is out of synch. Jack and Judy need two full-time weeks to get back on track, but they took a week's vacation in May and a few days at Easter time and now have only three days left, which they must save for a hunting trip in the fall. Even if they worked like dogs in their spare time, they won't catch up. Things will continue to go wrong. They will say they don't have time to produce their own food. They will say it is cheaper to buy food than to raise it. And in their situation they will be correct. They will give up and join the bowling league.

The fence should have been fixed in early spring. The goat should have been bred, have had a kid, and be giving milk. The manure in the shed should be on their yellow brick road of good intentions that they call a garden. The hens should have been butchered two years ago and their places taken with young, vigorous hens. The tiller should have been put in A 1 shape in April, ready to be put in cultivating use exactly and precisely when that clay dirt was at the mellow, soft state between too wet and too dry, when it would have made a fine, easily hoed seedbed. Then there would have been satisfaction in their work, pleasure in its success, and good food in the refrigerator.

There are precise times for planting and harvesting, and if you miss them, you miss the whole meaning of home food production. There are days when the soil is perfect for working and planting, and you must be ready. Once planted, the crops must be kept weeded, not when you feel like it, but when the garden demands it. There is the right day to pick your corn or peas. If you miss it, you might as well buy your vegetables from the wholesale distributor. There is the right day to pick a pear, and if you don't it will be grainy; the right day to pick a peach and if you wait, it will fall off the tree and bruise. When the ewes lamb, you better be home; when the strawberries are ripe, you better not be visiting City Cousin.

Losing the good taste of quality food because of ill-timing is not, in my opinion, the greatest tragedy. If you are one step behind Nature, you can work twice as hard as your neighbor who keeps up with her, and have nothing to show for it—and that *is* sad. A moment of prevention is worth two weeks of cure. Weed now and golf later, and you will have twice as much time to golf.

The only way successful backyard food producers get the work done and still have time for play is by making lists of "jobs to be done this week" and then systematically knocking them off one by one, 15 minutes before breakfast, a half hour at lunch, 2 hours of daylight saving time after dinner. I like to make lists. I'm a compulsive listmaker in fact, but unfortunately not a very compulsive knocker-off-er.

In Backyard Food Production, Timing Is Everything

Actually, I do not make lists of jobs in order to knock them off. I just want to get a firm idea of the size of the opposition. Without lists, I go around overwhelmed by the demands of good intentions. Work hangs over me, oozes out from under me, sneaks up behind me, looms up in front of me. I know not which way to turn, either to work or, what is more often the case, to avoid work.

But with lists made, I feel safer. It is much like the difference between having five goats securely tied in stalls or five goats cavorting around the neighborhood. In either case, the milking is yet to be done, but in the former case, it is I who can say when. A list stays tethered to the calendar. The individual jobs can't scatter away and hide behind the days that have passed. I can back away from a list, eye it from a distance, cover it with a picture, turn the light out over it, close the door on it. The work is all there, corralled on the list, and I can safely steal away and go fishing.

It is not a good idea to make lists in the spring. At least, do not take your spring lists seriously. They will be full of heady romance and wild exuberance. The lists you want to follow are the ones you make in the fall — fall lists are always permeated with the sober practicality you have learned after a tough summer. Here is one of my old spring lists, on the back of the April page of the calendar. It reads:

1. Build new barn
2. Stretch new fence
3. Plant trees
4. Fertilize pasture
5. Hatch toad eggs (honest, that's what it says)
6. Order weird corn seed
7. Write man in Canada for nude oats (I'm just reading what it says on the list)
8. Get tub to raise crawdads in

On the back of October, I find a sterner view of reality:

95

1. Patch roof of old barn and hang door
2. Mend old fence
3. Plant tree seeds where trees died
4. Buy hay
5. Make a sheep waterer out of crawdad tub
6. Cut wood
7. Grind feed

A project, once committed to paper and scrutinized for a few months, tends to lose its allurement. By the cold light of November, I know, if a little sadly, that I am not going to raise crayfish or hatch toads. Another advantage of lists is that a project decided upon in haste is left there on the paper to age a little. In January you may want to throw it away along with the other junk that the passing days have made obsolete.

Nevertheless, fairly accurate and helpful lists of projects can be made up for the coming year, the coming month, and the coming week, if you keep a garden diary as mentioned in the preceding chapter and use it to guide your scheduling. Studying the diary, you can easily draw up an outline of the coming year's work by listing all the necessary projects that must be done at specific times. Get a calendar that is blank on the back side of each page or that leaves room for writing on or under each numbered day. I don't have to do this as much now as I used to, because this part of my work list never changes much from year to year and it has kind of worked its way into the marrow of my bones and the rhythm of my life. But such a list would look like this for my own particular soil and climate:

January: (leave blank for the moment, nothing
              absolutely must be done in January)
February: (see above)
March: 1. Breed rabbit
              5-15. Tap maple trees
              10. Expect lambs
April: 1. Rabbits born

	5. Spray dormant oil on fruit trees
	10. Start plants in hotbed
	15. Graft fruit trees
	20. Turn sheep out to pasture
	25. Plant early vegetables, oats, and strawberry plants
May:	1-31. Continuous weed control as weeds germinate
	10. Peak of corn planting time
	12. Put composted chicken manure from coop along corn rows
	20. Set out tomatoes and other tender plants
	25. Peak of bean planting time
June:	1-30. Continue weeding as weeds germinate and/or spread mulch and manure
	1. Rabbit butchering should be completed
	12. New chicks
	15. Peak of strawberry harvest
	25. Harvest peas
	30. Pick cherries
July:	4. Cultivation/mulching completed
	10. Wheat ripe
	12. Summer raspberry peak
	20. Oats ripe
August:	10. Sweet corn harvest peak
	15. Tomato harvest peak
	25. Peach harvest peak
	30. Butcher broilers
September:	1. Melon harvest peak
	10. Butcher lamb
	25. Plant wheat
	30. Store onions and potatoes
October:	1. Fall raspberry peak and apple peak
	15. Harvest field corn and popcorn
	20. Cidermaking/apple harvest cleanup
November:	1. Clean up gardens for winter
	5. Finish raking and piling leaves for next year's mulch

6. Get wood hauled from woods before rains soften soil

10. Put ram with ewe

11. Butcher old hens as they begin molting

December: No "musts"

Next go back through the calendar and write down those yearly jobs that have to be done in a certain general season, or are best done during a certain season, but don't have to be done at a specific time in the life of plant or animal. These would include:

Pruning—February, March
Planting trees, vines, shrubs—March, November
Woodcutting—October through February, stopping when sap begins to rise
Mowing—May through September
Caring for bees and honey—May through October
Building construction, repair, and painting—August through November
Tool and machinery maintenance—December through February
Fence installation and repair—March, April

Now go back through the calendar again and list the recreational activities you want to participate in. Since mine are all seasonal, I have no trouble deciding where to schedule them:

Sundays in March and April—hunt Indian relics
Sundays from April 15 to May 15—bird watching/ wild flower hikes
Sundays from May 15 through August 15—play softball
Sundays in September and October—play football
Sundays and evenings in December and January as weather permits—ice hockey
Evenings in December—make Christmas presents out of wood
One Sunday in October—nut gathering

In Backyard Food Production, Timing Is Everything

Once you have this part of your schedule nailed down, you can pinpoint vacation dates, talk to your employer about taking time off without pay (trustworthy workers in rural areas often have such arrangements to allow them to tend to their little farms), and then put down new or unusual projects you want to try (like raising fish in the backyard) when they won't conflict with regular work.

As I look over this schedule, I suppose it seems terribly formidable, especially in addition to my regular workweek in an office. Actually, it flows along fairly smoothly, mostly because the whole family—four of us—pitch in to help. There are days when I think it would be nice to sit on an ocean beach and get terribly bored, but mostly I like it this way. I can't even say that I am well organized and disciplined because the seasons do the organizing and I *like* the work of producing my own food.

The enjoyment of seeing a little piece of land revolve harmoniously and fruitfully with the seasons is motivation enough for me to try to keep my timing sharp. But there is another secret to it, I think, and that is the variety of the work and the fact that each of the various food production projects are small in scale. We get finished with a specific job before it gets physically exhausting and/or boring. We are not trying to feed the world, but only ourselves with a little extra to trade, give to friends, or to sell.

Most new homesteaders and owners of Two Acre Edens go overboard. Their work becomes slavery, and in the process of trying to grow a "profitable" amount to sell, they may not get enough for themselves. I think of cane sorghum. I learned from a homesteader who put out two acres, dreaming of $2,000 profit plus all the syrup his family could eat. The wind blew the stalks over and even after grueling work under a September sun, they could make little headway trying to strip, cut, and trim the bent and tangled mess. An early frost caught them and ruined most of the crop.

I plant just two rows, each 200 feet long or so. In a pleasant morning's or evening's "work," our family and my sister's family strip the leaves off the stalks. Actually we gossip about all the goings-on in our neighborhood and just happen to get the sorghum stripped in the process. It's not work; it's fun. A few days later, we go to the field again, cut the stalks, trim off the tops, load up the pickup, and all drive down to the Amish farmer, who I think enjoys our fascination with his press and boiler almost as much as we do. Out of what may amount to a day's "work," each of our two families gets two to three gallons of syrup — more than we need.

Many homemakers like to can two or three bushels of tomatoes at a time and complain about what an awful job it is. We never do that. We do a little freezing and canning on many days, usually with two or more of us helping, often blanching a few pints of peas for freezing while cooking a batch to eat. There are only a few days in August when my wife really feels beat from preserving food all day.

Likewise, when I butcher chickens, I never do more than four and usually only two at a time. I don't much like to butcher but it's a snap to do only two. I'm not interested in getting work "over and done with" because this work is as much a part of my life as writing or playing softball. I butcher one pig or one lamb. People say I might as well butcher two while I'm at it. Two would become work for me. One is closer to play. This is why subsistence farming is enjoyable where commercial farming can be burdensome.

But rather than brag about myself, which isn't fair anyway because I have lots of help, I am going to brag about my sister Marilyn. From her and her husband's Two Acre Eden, she produces more food *for the amount of time spent* at it than any gardener I know. In fact she is so efficient with her time that she has become disgusting to the rest of us brothers and sisters who garden around her.

Little scenarios like this occur many times every year: It is July 30, and we have just finished eating our first big batch of full-season sweet corn from the garden. The phone rings. My wife looks at me. "Let me guess,"

I say. "That's Marilyn and she has already frozen 20 pints of corn." Carol picks up the phone. "Hello. Yes. Yes, we just got our first corn. Yes, it sure is good. What? You've already frozen 20 pints? I don't see how you do it!" Carol tries hard to sound amazed. Inwardly, she is cussing. What a burden to have a sister-in-law who always gets everything done before she does. But we are used to it. Marilyn starts with maple syrup in the spring and doesn't let up until after cider in the fall. And then she will call right after Halloween and inform us casually that she has her Christmas shopping finished already.

Nevertheless, she has something to brag about when it comes to food production. In what she calculates as an average of about an hour a day throughout the growing season, she produces the following amounts of food. Her garden plots are rather small, but she double-crops and makes successional plantings all season.

From vegetable plot number 1, size 50 feet by 15 feet, come the following preserved vegetables in addition to all her family (four older, hungry children) eats daily during the summer, spring, and fall.

1. Frozen peas—12 pints
2. Frozen beans—1 bushel
3. Canned beets—15 pints
4. Stored onions—1 bushel
5. Frozen leeks—6 pints
6. Frozen broccoli—6 pints
7. Frozen cauliflower—6 pints
8. Frozen lima beans—6 pints
9. Frozen carrots—12 pints

In addition, from this garden come 12 heads of lettuce and leaf lettuce for salads every day for four to five months, 12 heads of cabbage—6 early and 6 late—endive, spinach, radishes, salsify, scallions, and about 20 peppers.

From garden plot number 2, size 35 feet by 30 feet, come 180 ears of sweet corn, eaten fresh and some frozen

(20 pints), a bushel of popcorn, 30 quarts of different kinds of canned pickles, 3 pumpkins, and 6 sunflowers.

From garden plot number 3, 35 feet by 20 feet, come 4 bushels of tomatoes, a bushel of potatoes ("I can't grow potatoes," she says), about 40 muskmelons, about 20 watermelons (she plants 12 hills of the former and 6 of the latter), a bushel of winter squash, and from 1 zucchini plant, all the zucchini the family eats fresh plus 4 quarts frozen.

She has an asparagus bed only 10 feet by 2 feet from which she gathers spears every other day during the season for the table and freezes 4 pints ("the men in the family don't like asparagus very much"), 5 pints of rhubarb for spring pies and 7 quarts frozen for use through the year, 5 Concord grapevines that yield normally 1 bushel of grapes, 2 white Catawba vines that yield 1 peck of grapes, a cherry tree that yielded 42 quarts the last time it didn't freeze out but that "looks like it has 100 quarts on it this year," 4 apple trees that produce about a bushel each, a peach tree that when it doesn't freeze out yields 2 bushels of fruit. Her 2 strawberry beds, one 6 feet by 30 feet and the other 6 feet by 45 feet, yield about 75 quarts annually. A 6-foot by 15-foot row of red raspberries yields 20 quarts annually.

And that's far from all. She gathers enough hickory nuts in the woods every other year (the hickories don't produce every year here) to crack and pick out 12 quarts of nutmeats, which gives her 6 quarts to use per year. She also picks out a quart of black walnut nutmeats and a pint of wild hazelnuts. She makes her own maple syrup—18 pints last year—boiled off in the garage on an old gas stove her husband picked up for her that cost, I think, $16. She hunts a few mushrooms, enough for two meals of fall mushrooms and one of spring morels. She is a scrounger, trading labor or surplus food of her own for two gallons of sorghum molasses (from me) and corn for cornmeal. She says that 48 ears of field corn will make all the cornmeal her family normally uses. She has her own wheat for flour. She gathers free apples from neighbors or wild apples to make 20 gallons of cider and 12 quarts of pure juice, extra grapes from Grandpa for 20 quarts of juice, enough plums from my brother for 12 quarts canned, and enough of Grandpa's pears for 12 quarts canned. She fattens 1 pig a year in a pen in the yard for 100 pounds of pork, feeds out 12 broilers, and keeps 6 hens for eggs.

Oh yes, from the wild, she likes to gather a few elderberries, wild plums, black raspberries and black-berries, enough for immediate use, plus two pints each frozen and three quarts each in jelly. She also wangled a half-bushel of old-fashioned crab apples from a neighbor who doesn't use them and made spiced crab apples last year.

You shoppers who know the supermarket price of all this food can add the cost up and see what her labor has saved. She says the pig doesn't save much money at all, but tastes so much better than "boughten." What her food is worth is not what impresses me. It's the ease with which she does the work and the enjoyment she gets from it. And she agrees with me that the secret is not doing too much of any one thing, and spreading the work out over the entire year.

I took all this information from her over the phone. It is June 15. My peas are beginning to pod. She just called back to tell me she forgot the dandelion greens and winter onions she likes so well in early spring. Then she told me, as if it were an afterthought totally unpremeditated: "I'm freezing peas today. Yours ready yet?" I called her Fred and she hung up.

Chapter 11

Which Garden Catalog
Will First Win a Pulitzer . . .
for Fiction?

Every January I thumb through the new seed catalogs hoping to find examples of more creative ways to fudge the truth than I have found in previous years. Rarely am I disappointed. The prize winner this year—to which I give my Great Guffaw Award—goes to what I will nickname White Lie Nurseries in Tall Tale, Indiana. Although White Lie did not manipulate any really new half-truths, it did manage to offer the usual fabrications in a newer and more imaginative way.

I opened my White Lie catalog to a neat, apparently typed letter from a man I'll call Joe Doe, Jr. The letter read in part: "Dear Gene Logsdon: You and our other friends in your hometown (the name was given) have a special treat awaiting you in the pages of this all-new . . . ," etc., etc.

Isn't that nice. I don't know about his other friends in my hometown, but I've never heard of Joe before. Still, isn't it wonderful that a big nursery with customers all over the United States would spend the money on a computer to personalize a piece of promotional mail by inserting my name and hometown in the proper places on a form letter? My, my. Who says the computer makes numbers of us all?

But to continue the letter. "In response to requests from our customers throughout your state (name given) and other sections of the country we're introducing 'Pro Selection'—a new service which takes the guesswork out of buying mail order. Our professional nurserymen have pre-evaluated every variety and size of each item and selected the very best for shipping, planting, and assured growth. This means that you only have to look through the catalog and let us know which trees, shrubs, and plants you'd like to grow around your home in (town name supplied) and we'll take over from here. You'll be assured of receiving the very finest planting stock available—everything individually selected by professional nurserymen, carefully packed and shipped at the right planting time for (county name given)."

How sweet. A mail-order catalog that is going to tell me which plants will grow well right here in my little home-sweet-home climate. Right?

Wrong. That's what makes this little white lie an award winner. This is pure marketing genius. Mr. Doe never said that. He only said he would send me the plants I picked from his catalog and he'd send the size he had available at the time we usually plant in this neck of the woods. This is exactly what every mail-order catalog does, only much less. Ordinarily the customer can pick from a large number of varieties, the size he wants, and have it shipped at the time he wants. White Lie Nurseries has usurped these choices, reduced its service and made it sound as if it were doing the customer a favor. That calls for the biggest trophy ever to accompany a Guffaw Award. My congratulations to Mr. Doe, Jr. Next thing you know, he'll want to write a book on gardening.

Now accompany me on a trip through this catalog as I make my selections, as Mr. Doe's computer has instructed me, and see which selections the pros have pre-selected and pre-evaluated for my convenience. Ozark

Beauty everbearing strawberry is described as giving "extra heavy production." No everbearing strawberry has ever given me extra heavy production, least of all Ozark Beauty, in my climate. White Lie's pros list Surecrop strawberry as a late-maturing berry. Since when? But perhaps that was just an honest typing mistake. The catalog then lists for my selection a variety it calls New Sequoia. Since when? Sequoia is kind of new for Pennsylvania, but it is old in California.

On another page, Thornless Canby raspberries are described as "one of the largest, finest, and most popular raspberries." Take a poll. I bet you can't find one raspberry grower in 20 who ever heard of Thornless Canby. At least not around here.

Reference is made to Giant Latham raspberries. Lathams are not known for extra size. On the next page, White Lie's experts have selected for my needs a thornfree blackberry which I know will freeze out here, as will the boysenberry and the Lucretia dewberry the catalog offers. On another page, a "hardy persimmon" is offered. If the picture is to be believed (always a mistake), the persimmon is an oriental type and would also freeze out here. White Lie's experts pick Sugar Baby watermelon for us, an inferior variety for our soil. For peas, they list Early Alaska, the poorest tasting pea of the bunch in my opinion. Globe artichoke, which grows on the West Coast, gets considerable space. Beside it is advertised Jerusalem artichoke, which does grow here. It grows so well it has become a vicious weed in grain and soybean fields.

Elsewhere, White Lie reminds us that "there's a major advantage to buying from a leading grower like White Lie. Since there are no middlemen involved, there's no reshipping and danger of damage from constant handling—and no added costs."

Well, it's a very rare, large volume mail-order nursery (if any) that grows everything it ships. But White Lie is honest enough to admit that on another page, where it offers imported onion sets and says, "Nobody knows how to produce onions like the Dutch. That's why our experts

have imported these outstanding onion sets from Holland."
No middleman? Welllll, that depends on how you define
middleman. And I don't think Dutchmen know any more
about onions than Texans do.

But don't get me wrong. I'm not objecting to White
Lie's way with words. I wouldn't miss the yearly blizzard
of half-truths that come my way in the seed catalogs. We
gardeners like being lied to, in fact. We want to dream of
buying something new and different, the way some people
want to throw money away on horse races. That's how we
keep from going mad through the dismal days of winter.

The first thing a true-blue gardener looks for in the
latest catalog are the new varieties. Most new varieties are
no different or no better than the old ones and some are
even worse. Some aren't even new; in the lexicon of seed
catalog advertising, a variety is "new" for at least ten years,
and then it becomes "old reliable." Among the "new" varieties that always win our quick attention are the weird
crosses between plants that probably would not cross in
nature for 3 billion years. A few years ago the topato was
all the rage, a plant that reportedly grew tomatoes aboveground and potatoes on the roots. I have yet to see one of
these curiosities actually growing, but I keep waiting
eagerly for the first big display of topatoes in my supermarket. The next year news of the tomango warmed the
cockles of my heart — a cross between tomato and mango
with a taste that I agree with the advertising would have to
be "out of this world." Next it was celtuce, a cross between
celery and lettuce that a little boy tells me has "a taste
worse than either of 'em."

Some crosses are major successes, however. I think
of those little clementines in the supermarket, which are
crosses between oranges and tangerines. They are so good
and so expensive that you can eat right through a paycheck
without stopping and still be hungry.

My award for the weirdest, "sensational new" vegetable came in 1977, when horticulturists at Purdue University announced the "all-new melon-squash," describing it
cautiously as a vegetable "you may find suits your taste."

What may be may also not be. Who wants a melon that tastes like a squash or vice versa? I have trouble keeping my melons from tasting like squash now. I can think of only one all-new vegetable that would be worse — a cucumber-melon.

If melon-squash doesn't sound to your liking, or you can't find it yet in your favorite catalog, turn the page and contemplate those blue tomatoes. Or purple beans. How about a white strawberry? A yellow beet? An orange tomato?

There is no argument among tastes. Anything tastes good if you like it, even melon-squash. And since we will have progress whether we want it or not, I expect to see the following vegetables advertised some time in the future:

1. The Hickpumpkin: This new vegetable has the appearance of a hickory nut but weighs upwards of 50 pounds. Trees often need to be braced. Can be eaten raw or cooked. When ripe it falls from the tree. A forest of hickpumpkins in the fall sets up a weird drumming sound that can be heard for miles. God help the squirrel who decides to bury a cache of them for winter food.

2. The Thornaloupe: A cantaloupe with a very thorny rind to discourage groundhogs and small children.

3. The Redwood Gourd: A giant-size gourd with, yes, you guessed it, a hard, wooden shell. When ripe it can be hollowed and used for a garage.

4. Seedless Sweet Corn: The perfect variety for making corncob jelly.

5. The Gasless Bean: You've heard of the burpless cucumber. Well, now a navy bean for gas pain sufferers everywhere. By developing a bean with a thin endosperm, scientists say all gases are given off as the beans are baked and before they are eaten. Best for outdoor cookery.

6. The American Carrot: At last, but unfortunately too late for the bicentennial year, a red, white, and blue-striped carrot. Can be dried and used for Christmas tree ornaments.

7. The Moodmelon: Here's a novelty every gardener will want to grow. This melon changes colors with your

emotions. If you are feeling low, it turns blue. If you are scared, it turns whitish yellow. If you are angry, it turns red. But like every watermelon, when you think it is ready to eat, it turns green, and when you wait a little longer it turns rotten.

8. The Popcherry: What every cherry grower has always dreamed of. This new cherry has been crossed with popcorn and has a seed that, after ten seconds in a bird's stomach, explodes.

Yep, all this and much more awaits us in the future. In the meantime, psst . . . does anybody have the address of the seed company selling melon-squashes?

Such creations sound very silly, and are, but some of the *real* items you run across in unscrupulous mail-order catalogs sound nearly as weird. I was appalled recently to find a plant called the "amazing climbing vine peach" and another named "tasty novelty mango melon." In very fine print the wary reader might have noticed that both of these sensations were the same plant *(Cucumis Melo,* Chito Group), but I wonder how many trusting souls sent for both offerings. The "climbing vine peach" was described as "just yummy fresh from the vine, in salads, pickled or preserved . . . orange size, uniquely flavorful juicy 'peaches' with a taste somewhere between cantaloupe and mango." Somewhere indeed. Under the mango melon melodrama, the advertising copy wandered a bit more poetically, but perhaps slightly closer to the truth: "These unique ornamental fruits are mini-melons tasting like a cantaloupe to some, mangos to others, and can be seasoned to taste for fresh eating." That's as brilliant a piece of Vague Writing as the last presidential speech.

But the advertiser did not lie. Not exactly anyway. The scientific name was there for all to see, if you squinted hard enough. In this case even the *complete* scientific name was given. On another page, there was advertised a "Pie-perfect bush cherry *(Prunus)."* *Prunus* is the genus name for all the cherries, plums, apricots, and related ornamental bushes — about 200 species, plus innumerable strains, crosses, and hybrids. To call a bush cherry *Prunus* is no more specific than calling a whale a mammal.

The *Prunus* genus embraces many fruits—some good, some merely edible. That's why it has become the happy hunting grounds of the circus barkers who sell wonder fruits. Familiarize yourself with some of the main branches of the genus, so you know what you're buying.

Group I

Prunus avium—common sweet cherry
P. Cerasus—common sour cherry
P. Armeniaca—common apricot
P. domestica—common plum
P. insititia—Damson plum

Group II

P. tomentosa—Nanking cherry or Hansen's bush cherry
P. americana, P. hortulana, P. nigra, P. Munsoniana—all native wild American plums
P. angustifolia—Chickasaw plum, mainly of the Southeast
P. Besseyi—sand cherry or western sand cherry
P. maritima—beach plum of the eastern coast
P. pumila—also called sand cherry, but much rarer than *P. Besseyi*. It is found in the Great Lakes region, while *P. Besseyi* is native of the dry northern Plains.
P. salicina—Japanese plum

These are not by far all the main branches of the *Prunus* genus and each of these is divided into numerous subspecies. What I have designated as Group I are the trees grown principally for fruit. Group II are more or less bushes, grown principally as ornamentals. These particular ornamentals do have some food value however, especially in climates where ordinary fruits won't survive, and potentially may have very significant food value. Operating somewhere between the real and the potential, the circus barkers mix fact and fancy in a way that is deceiving, if you can't decipher the adjectives properly.

We're seeing more quackery in plant merchandising these days because of the increased interest in all kinds of fruits. With good named varieties in short supply, unscrupulous growers are unloading junk that has accumulated in their nurseries. Most often the mail-order merchandisers who have little more than a catalog buy this stuff up at cheap prices and make a profit selling to naive, ignorant new gardeners and homeowners who are caught up in the trend toward growing their own food.

When a catalog offers a "sensational new bush plum" that is not a named variety or has no specific scientific name identifying it, what's most likely being offered are seedlings that may or may not come true to parent stock and that may or may not possess good eating quality.

Among the bush fruits most frequently encountered in nursery catalogs is the Hansen's bush cherry, sometimes called the sand cherry *(Prunus Besseyi)*. The Dr. Hansen it is named after certainly never intended to sell the public shoddy material, but worked long and hard to select the best wild bush fruits that would survive on the dry, cold Plains, where regular fruits wouldn't. The fruit is smaller and not as tasty as a regular sour cherry. On the Plains where no other cherry will grow, it has advantages, but it is extremely susceptible to brown rot and therefore rather impractical to grow in more humid eastern regions.

The Nanking cherry *(Prunus tomentosa)* is another bush cherry often encountered in catalogs. Gurney Seed and Nursery Company, Yankton, SD 37079, gives away small plants free with orders, which is how I got mine, and which, I think, gives some idea of its actual value. Though quite small, the Nanking cherry is prolific and actually very nearly equal to the Montmorency sour cherry in taste. Where regular sour cherries can't be grown, it may be a suitable alternative, though it too is susceptible to brown rot, though not as much as Hansen's bush cherry.

The latest rage among purveyors of the unusual is the Manchurian bush apricot *(Prunus Armeniaca* var. *mandshurica)*. It is touted as being the "hardiest apricot in the world"—which it probably is.

The home gardener, however, should try the named varieties that have been developed by crossing the Manchurian with other regular apricots. Manchu is one that has proven somewhat satisfactory for colder regions. Scout is another one that has been fairly successful. It was developed at the research station at Morden in Manitoba. (Scout and Manchu are available from Gurney's, among others. Farmer Seed and Nursery, Faribault, MN 55021, sells newer cold-resistant apricots like Sungold and Moongold.)

Buying plums can be even more confusing than apricots or cherries because there are more varieties and strains. For example, the Damson plums are considered "legitimate" tree fruit, but most of them are too tart for eating out of hand. This characteristic is generally true of the bush or ornamental plums too. If you live on the East Coast where the beach plum grows well, you may be just as well off with it as with a Damson, especially if you can find a local nursery that sells a selected named strain of beach plum. In its limited range, the beach plum is highly regarded for jams and jellies.

Folks who live in the South and Southeast believe the Chickasaw plum *(Prunus angustifolia)* is the equal of the beach plum when it comes to good jams and jellies. But today it's more difficult to find a good one growing wild in the fencerows. If you can find a pure strain, the fruits are often good to eat out of hand, in addition to making excellent jellies.

Other wild native plums, particularly *Prunus americana* and *P. hortulana* are very flavorful for jams and jellies. A few strains were selected and named years ago and were offered by nurseries up until about 1940. Terry, Gold, Queen, Nellie, Blanche, Hammer, and Hawkeye were some of the better known varieties, but they are not available anymore. Research stations have even bulldozed out their clones of native plums.

In the wonder fruit catalogs, you often see Manchurian plum or even Siberian plum sometimes labeled *"Prunus salicina hybrid."* That Latin label is almost meaningless — all it tells you is that the plant is Japanese plum *(P. salicina)* crossed with most anything. Most generally though, it denotes — or should — some hybridized offspring of a hardy seedling that came from Harbin, Manchuria, about 30 years ago and has been grown experimentally ever since. Because of seedling variability, what you actually get may vary markedly from the "juicy, super hardy, exotic, delicious" wonder fruit advertised. But you might be lucky.

Hybrid "cherry plums" are now offered even in trustworthy catalogs. Choose named varieties like Sapalta or Compass (available from Farmer Seed and Nursery, among others), where you have assurance of some quality. Cherry plums are hybrids of *Prunus cerasifera* crossed with other (usually Japanese) plums. Another name for *P. cerasifera* is myrobalan plum. Its chief value is as a rootstock for apricots and other stone fruits. But some strains make nice ornamentals, and some produce fruit worthy of the backyarder's attention.

It would certainly be a mistake to ignore the humble little bush fruits. In addition to being an alternative where no other fruits will grow, these bush fruits carry the genetic potential to develop small, quality fruiting plants that are easy to take care of. But know what you are buying.

The *Prunus* genus of plants is not the only one the catalog circus barkers use to take your money under questionable pretenses. *Viburnum trilobum* is a common landscaping bush. Because of its enormous number of attractive red berries, it has become known colloquially as the "highbush cranberry." That kind of name is too much for the flimflammers to pass up. In one catalog I see, next to a color photo of *V. trilobum*'s "gorgeous scarlet" berries, a picture of roast turkey and cranberry sauce, and a happy caption: "Makes Any Meal a Holiday Feast." Then follows the usual glowing misinformation: ". . . a blaze of fiery red and orange in fall . . . huge clusters of scarlet cranberries ripen in late July and stay plump and juicy right through winter . . . for sauces, relishes, jellies, preserves . . ." The word cranberry is not even in quotes.

Viburnum trilobum is not a cranberry, nor do its berries taste like cranberries. The fruit is edible, but the tip-off to the truth is right in that hymn of praise, "stay plump and juicy right through winter." *Even the birds don't like them much, or they'd eat them long before winter was over.*

You can use that same method to judge the flavor of autumn olive berries. There is great variation in the taste of autumn olive berries from bush to bush. Even though the plant is often advertised as being great for jams and jellies, some are and some aren't. If you try to find out by tasting, the astringent berries will soon pucker your mouth to the point where you can't taste anything. Instead, watch which ones the birds like best. If they won't eat the berries, you can be sure they're too tart for jelly. Good ones make a jelly that tastes like currants, and some will develop a ripe-plum flavor when dead ripe, if the birds haven't eaten them by then.

But a good rule to follow when looking at wonder fruit ads is to beware of fruits about which the advertiser can think of nothing better to say than "makes good jellies and preserves." As Midwestern farmwives know, you can make preserves out of watermelon rinds and a fairly tasty jelly out of corncobs — if you use enough sugar.

Gardeners are their own worst enemies when it comes to buying "new" plants. As I mentioned in chapter 3, they are suckers for every fast-growing tree a nurseryman can stock and are ready to believe the most unbelievable claims of exotic and unusual beauty.

Invariably, buying fast-growing trees is a bad mistake. Fast-growing trees are almost always inferior for home landscapes. They are either short-lived, weak limbed, dirty, ugly, or all of the above. People plant them for quick shade or screening and battle their bad habits all the days of their lives. The pity of all this is that a good shade tree, say a white oak or sugar maple, grows surprisingly fast after establishing a good root system, until it reaches a height of about 20 feet, at which time it will certainly shade as well as, for example, a Lombardy poplar, which usually dies at about 12 to 16 years of age and falls on your neighbor's fence. The slow growth of oaks and maples after that time is actually an advantage, since most trees tend to become crowded in a typical home landscape situation anyway.

Another reason novelty will always remain in style in garden catalogs is the gardener's desire to one-up his fellow hoe swingers. That's Fred, my neighbor. Fred likes to roll words like *Cucumis Melo,* Chito Group off his tongue in my direction or to plant trees that grow "roof high in just a month." He was the first in our area to plant a multi-flora rose hedge, and he still hasn't gotten rid of it completely, nor have we. He once grew a "special clone" of one fast-growing poplar tree which, so he bragged to me, would grow ten feet a year. It did. He had planted it too close to the house, however, and it was threatening to push the eave trough up in line with the chimney. So he cut the tree down. Four more sprang up from the roots. Literally sprang. When they threatened to chin themselves on the eave, he cut them down too. Then 17 sprouts came up. At first he thought he had discovered the ultimate answer to fuel supply limits, but even after drying for three years, the wood would barely burn unless sliced in slivers about the size of toothpicks.

Nature has spent eons perfecting a few plants for every environment. Listen to her, not the circus barkers. Her words will win no Pulitzers, but Pulitzers will not put food on your table either.

Chapter 12

Subsistence Living
in a Technological Society:
In Case You Don't Want
to Come a Long Way, Baby

When city people retreat to the country, they look upon it as a step backward in time. Perhaps inspired by dim memories of childhood days spent on a farm, or disenchanted by the faults of modern technology, they see themselves adopting Grandfather's ways and Grandfather's tools and achieving a simpler way of life. At least their budget problems will be simpler, they think. Grandfather didn't need cash on the barrelhead every day. Nor will they.

They will learn how to live off the land, too: raise their own food, chop their own firewood, pump their own water, build their own roofs, sing their own songs. Subsist. That's what they will do. Subsistence living, followed quickly by joy, peace, and paradise.

Nonsense. To begin with, Grandfather's tools weren't all that simple, and furthermore, his way of life wasn't any happier than ours. Subsistence farming meant hard work, rewarded by mere survival. Grandfather strove to avoid any part of that in favor of all the niceties of civilization he could afford.

However, if you want to try to play "Subsistence"

(Parker Brothers will probably have a game out by that name pretty soon) as a sort of sport on your Two Acre Eden, you will have embarked upon one of those "fascinating hobbies," and you may even save some money.

The trick is to select, with the better view of hindsight, the best of the past (technology threw it all out in favor of the new) and the best, ecologically speaking, of the present and combine the two to achieve your goals.

I see, from my hammock, my beautiful wife, dressed in a swimsuit, pushing a wheeled cultivator between the rows of sweet corn. You cannot combine the old and the new much better than that.

The wheeled cultivator is the perfect tool for the moderately large garden. It cultivates faster and with much less effort than the hoe, breaks up the ground, and pulls out the weeds just as well as any motorized ring-pistoned roarer, never wears out (mine dates back 65 years), and always starts at the first push.

And is that wife pushing her cultivator a picture of degraded womanhood, kept in a state of servitude? Definitely not. She pushes voluntarily. It is more comfortable to get a suntan while in motion than to lie still on the ground and bake. Besides, she has discovered that the cultivator is a marvelous way to keep legs trim and stomach muscles strong. She needs to spend no money on reducing fads.

The old and the new. Accomplishing practical purposes without the useless expenditure of money. That's modern subsistence living. The only kind that works.

Down at the bicycle shop in our town the other day, I ran into a man for whom a monument should be raised.

"Don't own a car at all anymore," he said, while showing me his bicycle built for two. "This is our 'sedan.' My wife has her own bicycle, I have another one, and both of our kids have their own. Good bicycles."

"You don't own a car?" I asked in disbelief.

"Nope. Had two of them. It was awful. I found that I was spending about half my time worrying about car payments, repairs, insurance, inspections. It was always something, and one day I realized that automobiles were inserting themselves into my consciousness so much, my brain wasn't free to work on matters that are really important to me." He paused, looked at me piercingly, afraid I would not understand, afraid I would reveal, with a humoring smile, that I thought he was some kind of oddball. I told him he was the sanest man I'd met all week.

"We made the transition cautiously, over a two-year period. We knew we could save an awful lot of money—two cars cost us $10,000, but four bikes cost $800 and no interest. But we also knew that riding bicycles instead of cars would require some physical hardships and a few aggravations—like cold weather or getting caught in the rain. We also knew that we would need a car sometimes. I felt that if we planned everything correctly, we could rent a car for trips and still save money. And that has turned out to be correct."

"Do you ride your bicycle to work?"

"Oh yes. I get there quicker than when I drove a car. These bicycles are really marvelous now. Mine has ten speeds—ten gears, and in the lowest one, I can pedal up steep hills with little effort. In the top gear, I can go 60 miles per hour. Easily. The record is 128 mph. The most fun is to pass cars on the highway. Drivers do a double take and check their speedometers. But bicycling can be dangerous on a busy highway. Not the bicycling, but the cars."

"How does your wife like not having a car? Who gets the groceries in January?" I asked.

"Well, we went into this slowly. First, we had to live where my work and stores were fairly close by. We have everything delivered that there's a delivery service for. Then, since we were not going to be needing the garage for cars, I used part of it to build a walk-in freezer and cooler. Into it go lots of fruits and vegetables that we raise. We buy meat and other food in quantity and store it in the big freezer. Buying in bulk not only saves grocery trips, but saves money. No, it'll be a while before I buy another car."

"How much money do you save a year?"

"Oh, I don't know. What is good exercise worth?

Or rather what is overweight going to cost you? But I could exercise some other way, maybe. You save an unknown amount of money by not going a lot of places you otherwise might. I'll put it this way. The whole change we've made saves us $1,000 outright, solid. There are more savings, but they are canceled by our vacation trips, which, if we don't bike them, cost us a rented car. There are a few taxi and bus fares we wouldn't have to pay if we had a car, that sort of thing. But this year I've had nearly $1,000 to put in the bank that I never had before. And we also feel better physically."

I have mounted a soapbox at my place to get rid of the car and buy four bicycles. So far no luck. I can't even persuade my wife to trade in the car for a pickup truck— yet. I know so many things I could get free for Two Acre Eden if I had a truck. Manure, mulch, sawdust, rocks, used lumber for building, firewood, and all kinds of handy junk. Begging and scavenging with a truck is another form of modern subsistence living. A highly artistic form. Observing a friend of mine who does have a pickup, I can say without qualification that the right man with a truck at the right place at the right time can get, very reasonably, everything from an old one-lane bridge to 5 million rusty cement nails.

To play a good game of Subsistence, you need to know how much human life two acres of land is capable of supporting. Our place held more or less constantly:

Two adults and two children.

One modest three-bedroom house and oversized garage.

One garden shed and one small barn. The barn can accommodate 12 to 25 chickens, 3 cats, 2 families of rabbits, and either 2 pigs or 2 lambs.

About one acre of grass or hay, depending on how often I cut it.

About 170 trees from 2 to maybe 60 years old. The mix is about one-third conifer and two-thirds deciduous, including an orchard of five apple trees, eight peach, five cherry, one nectarine, and three pear.

About 300 bushes—200 ornamental bushes and 100

or so various kinds forming a hedge around the property. There are also 10 blueberry bushes, 200 feet of raspberry canes, and a strawberry patch that yields 100 quarts a year.

Various small flower gardens.

About a quarter-acre in vegetables. From this much land could come all our vegetable needs for the year, just as our orchard and berries provide us with all the fruits we need. I could easily raise more of either. In winter we would still have to buy lettuce for salads. We also buy onions and potatoes, not because I couldn't raise enough to last, but because I am too lazy to build proper storage bins for them. In addition to what we eat fresh, we freeze sweet corn, string beans, peas, and broccoli in quantity. Also some zucchini and other vegetables. Cucumbers are pickled; tomatoes canned. We freeze lots of peaches because we think they make the best frozen fruit. Also some strawberries, raspberries, and blueberries. The latter two freeze well; strawberries lose too much flavor.

Based on my experiences (and a lifetime of scrounging a living on the farm), I am convinced that if I were equipped to irrigate my two acres and if I cut down all or most of the nonfood trees and bushes, I could raise not only all our fruits and vegetables plus enough grain for bread, and honey for a sweetener, but also grow the forage and grain for the livestock that could keep us in milk, meat, and eggs. It would take all the agricultural know-how available to me and a little luck, but it could be done. I am using my two acres only to half-capacity and I am half of the way there. Not wasting an inch of ground, I could provide everything except salt, spices, soap, and fuel. Actually I could make soap from animal tallow and wood ashes. But I would need a well-managed woodlot of at least four acres from which to cut enough wood to keep us warm all winter. And by now, I would be working every minute I was home.

Even if I had the woodlot, I'd lose the Subsistence game because I do not have my own water yet; neither well, nor creek, nor spring, nor cistern. I have to depend on "city" water (ours fortunately comes from deep wells and tastes good), so I am at the mercy of the Establishment. If I don't toe the line, they can always literally turn my water off. So as any true self-subsister, I crave a well, which I could dig, or a cistern, which I could build, or a pure bubbling spring, which I can only dream about. When you have seen how the old farms in eastern Pennsylvania harness never-failing springs to provide a constantly flowing water system throughout house and barn, powered completely by gravity and operating without failure for 100 years, then you know the true meaning of selecting the very best of the old.

I would like to have a cistern again. That sounds positively ridiculous, but I'll enumerate the advantages of a cistern so you can understand the wisdom of it. When we lived in our woodland cabin for four years (and learned more than we cared to know about subsistence living), we depended on a cistern for all our household water. (We got drinking water at the nearest gas station in a big glass jug.)

Rain water is so soft, you need very little soap in the bathtub. Your hair, washed in rain water, positively shines no matter what shampoo you use. Nor do you have to throw a bunch of mysterious polluting enzymes into your washer to get your clothes soft and downy. Diapers washed in rain water need no help from strong detergents to come clean, and dried in the fresh air and sunshine, they suddenly don't cause diaper rash anymore. Water pipes won't rust as fast from the cistern as from the well. Plants grow better with rain water than with any other kind. And, of course, you don't need a water softener. And you don't have to be overly polite to the water company officials in town if a water shortage develops in your neck of the woods.

All you have to worry about is dry weather.

I don't know why I am trying to sell cisterns. But I feel there are things more people ought to know about, so that in a crisis they understand there is more than one alternative.

Cisterns have fallen into disrepute because they are not as convenient as tap water, take a little care and bother, and force you to conserve water. The latter is something city people must learn, anyway. They have wasted water so wantonly that the practice is now catching up with them.

The secret of good cistern water is never to allow summer rains of June, July, and August to flow into it. Hardly anyone knows this anymore, even people who have cisterns and who complain that their water gets a little stagnant in hot weather. (A condition that can be cured by dumping a little lime into the cistern.) A cistern should be large enough to hold a sufficient supply of fall, winter, and spring rains to last through the summer, with a little care. When I was a kid on the farm, we eagerly awaited the first, hard fall rain. After it fell, we were allowed to *fill* the bathtub for our Saturday night bath. In summer, we were limited to five inches in the bottom of the tub.

Anyway, when the first rain falls after a prolonged dry spell, you do not let the first water off the roof into the cistern. You wait till the roof is washed off. Downspouts are equipped with little gadgets that direct the flow into the cistern or out onto the lawn.

The water that does go into the cistern should flow through filters of charcoal, which can be placed right in the tile under the downspouts over a wire screen. You must change the charcoal every year or two. Screens must cover all openings that lead to the cistern. Otherwise, rats and mice will fall into it sooner or later.

Theoretically, cisterns should not have to be cleaned out. But once every seven or ten years we always found a good cleaning to be worthwhile.

So much for useless knowledge. But if everyone living in New York had been brought up on cistern water, New York would never have a water problem.

The true self-subsister has a well and he yearns for a windmill. A windmill, kept oiled, will outlast at least ten electric pumps, will indeed last just about forever unless a tornado ties it into a knot. You can still buy them: The Heller-Aller Company, Napoleon, OH 43545; Aermotor Division, Valley Industries, Inc., P.O. Box 1364,

Conway, AK 72032; and Dempster Industries, Inc., 711 South 6th Street, Beatrice, NB 68310.

If you can find a farmer who will part with his, you may get a used windmill cheaper. My brother-in-law got one this way. At a great expense of time and energy —not to mention danger—he moved it to his pond and attached it to a well in hopes that the wind would keep the pond full of water. It didn't. "Oh, actually, I didn't care so much about that," he explained. "I just wanted to have a windmill again. I grew up listening to one, and, well, it's a good sound."

As cherished antiques and as practical cattle waterers, windmills will never go completely out of style. There is something just too beautiful about making the wind work for you without having to pay a serivce charge. And there is poetry in the blades whirling against the sunset. Of course, if the wind won't blow when you need water, your poem will have some lines that rhyme with damn.

It is unfortunate that many people who have wells have discarded their hand pumps and rely on electric motors to get water out of the ground. No electricity, no water.

For selecting the best of the past and combining it with the best of the present, a fireplace is hard to beat. The human spirit has preserved the fireplace against all the blandishments of technology. Man cherishes the aesthetics of the open hearth and gets the practical side advantages for free. It's fun to gaze into the flames, to meditate alone or hoist a stein with hearty friends before the flickering light; it is also nice to know that if there was a power failure, you wouldn't freeze to death.

We had an excellent fireplace in our log cabin. There was never a wisp of smoke in the room, no matter how large or smoky my fire. The fireplace was huge. I didn't have to cut logs up very much; I could burn anything I could carry.

The fireplace was equipped with a crane, an iron arm, anchored in the stones on the left side, that could be swung out over the fire. From a hook on the end of it, we could hang a cast-iron pot, and we often cooked stews and soups just as easily as we could on the stove. On the right side of the fireplace was an oven, under which you could shove hot coals. It was very hard to keep a constant heat in the oven, but it was fun to prepare a meal this way occasionally. And it was comforting to know that we could survive a crisis that way—so long as we had something to cook. Our change-of-pace meal went like this: I'd dig up some potatoes, encase each one in clay, and bury them in the burning wood coals. Carol would hang a pot of ham and beans on the crane. A tray of biscuits went in the oven. Maybe we'd pop some corn. For dessert we'd roast marshmallows. We didn't have a cent in those days, but we haven't lived any better since.

The weakness of a fireplace is that most of the heat is lost up the chimney. That's why we, like so many others, eventually purchased a wood stove.

With the rise in utility bills and the uncertainty over fuel supplies, the wood stove has become very popular on Two Acre Edens that are large enough to contain some woodland. Even urbanites, especially those with access to free wood, are buying stoves for backup heating. In our experience, if you have to buy your wood, you don't save any money, though it is perhaps more secure to have a stack of wood behind the garage than to depend on electricity that some power beyond your control can turn off on you. Even when you have your own wood, you may not save any money during the period when you are first starting out to provide your own heat. There's a joking list of costs incurred from heating with wood that is making the rounds. I don't know who originated the list—I've seen several versions—but it makes the point. Good old neighbor Fred, who sneers at our wood stove because he has bought stock in the utility company, handed me one list that goes sort of like this:

Costs to Heat House with Wood

Chain saw	$300
Ax	$15

Wedges	$20
Splitting maul	$20
Mechanical splitter	$200
Annual repairs and new chain for saw	$50
Wood stove	$700
Stovepipe	$500
Flue installation (including fixing leak where pipe goes through roof)	$600
	(still leaks)
Restoration and repair of old chimney	$1,500
Repair of house after chimney fire	$12,000
Pickup truck	$7,000
Repair of truck after tree falls on it	$3,000
Doctor bills for injuries while cutting wood	$400
Poison ivy lotion	$5
Cost of redecorating living room after soot and smoke have ruined everything	$6,000
Plus new rug	$1,500
Divorce proceedings and settlement	$35,000
Revenue from 5 cords of wood	$400
Profits approximately	$-70,000

Actually, the situation is not quite that bad. Most of the equipment you will accumulate on your homestead in the course of time anyway, and much of the expense can be prorated over many years. A good wood stove will last as long as you will. Even a chainsaw, properly cared for, ought to be dependable for seven years. And you can buy used pickups that will last many years if you don't use them hard.

The trick to making wood heating really pay is to go into it seriously—for a lifetime. As long as your stove is only an afterthought, a backup for conventional heat, or a conversation piece, then it is in reality a toy or a luxury on the par with having a bar in the basement, and you can expect it to cost you money, not save any.

But a well-planned commitment to wood heating is something else. It took us many years to get there, but we were finally able to invest in ten acres of woodland. The major side benefit from this investment was all the wood we will ever need to heat the house—wood that normally would go to waste. With our wood stove, we supply about 90 percent of our home heating and have lowered our electric bill (our "backup" heat is electric) by exactly $400, calculated in 1978's cost per kilowatt. As the price of electricity soars, we feel that in the rest of our lifetime, we will save a significant amount of money. On the other hand, if we had to buy wood at $80 a cord (and rising) I don't think there would be any cash savings, or very little.

There are other dividends from wood heating that are not easy to calculate. Cutting wood happens to be an enjoyable exercise for me—now that I am properly equipped with a modern chain saw. I don't like chain saw noise, but the old crosscut saw is a man-killer if you have to cut *all* your wood with it. I also have an old, tractor-powered circular saw that is far more efficient in cutting up wood to stove length than the chain saw. Anyhow, I like to cut wood in the winter. Without this outlet, I would probably sit in front of the TV and get fat.

We have found that our house is supremely more comfortable to live in during cold weather when you can come in from the cold outdoors and sit down right next to the stove in 85 degree heat, if you want to. Modern central heating systems or electric room-by-room systems simply do not provide a *warm* place to sit, especially when you try to save fuel by keeping the thermostat set at 68.

A wood stove is very handy for keeping the coffee-pot hot and doing small cooking jobs. You can save electricity appreciably if you don't have to switch on a 220-volt burner every time you want a cup of tea.

As to what kind of stove you should buy, I have to say after an inordinate amount of homework and no little experience, that you might as well ask me what kind of car to buy. You gets what you pays for. The general attitude among experts these last years has been that the cast-iron, airtight stoves are the best. But among experienced users, this attitude is now questioned sharply. I have such a stove—cast-iron and airtight, or almost airtight—and I like it very much. But airtight stoves have a problem. If you burn wood slowly and "efficiently," you make a lot of creosote to foul the flue and chimney and precipitate chimney fires. Cheaper, nonairtight stoves burn more wood, but make less creosote. You can only avoid heavy creosote buildup with airtight stoves by running them hot, that is with plenty of air, at least two hours every day. So what do you gain? If you have the wood, it may be just as "efficient" overall (and less dangerous) to burn a cord or two more of wood per year. I have good friends who heat their "front" rooms and do *all* their winter cooking on an ancient, cheap, small Franklin-type stove they purchased for $25. They watch over the stove carefully, knowingly adjusting it to every whim of the burning wood, and I've about concluded that they heat just as efficiently as I do with a deluxe, airtight, superduper $700 parlor stove.

As to whether cast iron or steel makes the best stove, there is no easy answer. Cast iron cracks if there is a flaw in the casting or if mistreated, and steel warps if the gauge is too thin. A reputable company is worth 1,000 advertising slogans and an *intelligent* satisfied user worth 10,000 words of advice.

Whatever, I think there's too much worry spent over the stove and not enough over the installation. I don't know how many experts or stove merchants (there's a difference) I asked about venting my stove through the fireplace. None could or would give me definite, guaranteed answers. I just had to go ahead and do it. I closed up the fireplace opening with a piece of steel plating, designing my own clamps to hold it against the facing bricks of the fireplace. I ran the stovepipe about a foot through the steel plate into the fireplace, so that the end of the pipe comes just below the damper of the fireplace. The pipe actually slants downward a little, the stove outlet being a little higher than the fireplace, but it draws very well anyway. I jammed insulation around the steel plate to make it as airtight as possible.

This is a very cheap way to vent a stove compared to making a new chimney or running fluepipe up through a roof. In the latter case, be sure you have someone who knows how to do that properly before you go too far into wood heating. It isn't all as easy as the stove merchants sometimes make it out to be. For example, the way I have 'described (which works fine for me) is considered the least-desirable way to vent a stove into a fireplace. It's better to vent the stove to the flue above the fireplace opening.

I worried about heat scorching the floor underneath the stove. I found this to be only a very minor concern. As long as there are at least two inches of ashes in the firebox, very little heat radiates downward to the floor. I built an effective and fairly cheap safety pad with a piece of plywood of the right size covered with fireproof asbestos paper, and overlaid that with roof slates that I got used for next to nothing and that look fairly presentable even in a living room. I set the pad right on the rug, to my wife's consternation, but in spring when we took out the stove, the rug underneath looked no worse for the weight after a vacuuming or two.

There are no walls within two feet of the stove, so we didn't have to worry about protection from the heat there. But a wall relatively close to a stove is a reason to worry until you protect it correctly. There are many books to guide you and reputable stove manufacturers make sure you get the message, but if all these sources of information elude you, talk to your local fire chief. He will have plenty to say about wood stoves, usually from a dour point of view.

Ideally, a house should be built with wood heating in mind. Then there isn't all the gerrymandering around most of us have to do. And safety can be properly built-in. If you are in that situation, that is building a house to be heated by wood, check out wood *furnaces* as well as stoves. Old farmhouses that I'm quite familiar with are still heated with wood furnaces, and in my estimation they are heated so much more efficiently than any wood stove can do. And with less work. I was raised in such a house and was never so glad as when Dad put in a stoker coal system. But looking back, I know now a wood furnace is a better way than a wood stove.

Subsistence Living in a Technological Society

You are wondering why I do not give equal space to various systems of solar heating? Certainly nothing combines the old and the new any better. I will leave opinionated methods of how to use the sun to stay warm in cold weather to homesteaders who live farther south— where such systems will sooner prove practical. Where I live, we can go 30 days without enough sunshine to make the snow sparkle. Here in the North, think of solar heating as a way to heat water in the summertime. I don't see it —yet—for dependable house heating in winter.

Ever since the big power blackout in the Northeast, kerosene lanterns have been selling briskly. Get a couple for your Two Acre Eden. For six dollars or less you can buy the collected wisdom of centuries. So long as coal oil and kerosene are made, the lantern will never wear out.

I often find myself gardening in the dark with my flickering lantern beside me. Yes, the neighbors think I'm nuts. I generally tend to the barn chores in the dark, too, and a lantern beats a flashlight all hollow. Partly for sentimental reasons. As a boy, I used to run a trapline along a creek in the middle of the night. It was a little scary for a boy alone in the dark. I always carried a lantern—a bit of security and civilization against the evils that walketh in the night.

If you are lucky enough to own a Two Acre Eden that is actually larger, say ten acres, a woodlot can be a wonderful asset when playing Subsistence. Not only will wood warm you twice—once cutting it and once burning it—but you will find many other uses for your homemade lumber that make it worth its weight, if you've checked prices at the lumberyard recently.

The garden is always demanding some kind of trellis. Raspberry canes need braces, pole beans need poles, grapes need an arbor, blueberries need frames for screening out birds, tomatoes need stakes, gourds need trellising. Clotheslines need poles, fences need posts, barns need pillars, chickens need roosts, fruit trees need supports. The demand is endless. If you have to buy wood for these purposes, the cost adds up. If you have woods, you need only an ax and a saw. Even if you do not have woods but have planted too many trees on your property—as almost everyone does—you can keep yourself supplied with stakes as you cut down the overcrowding trees.

Woodcutting used to be a really onerous task. The farmers of the last century knew how to avoid some of the hard work because of their expert knowledge of wood and the tools used to cut it. They had axes for every operation, not just one kind as most of us have today. And they kept their axes and saws extremely sharp—an art all but lost now. Unless you have worked with an ax or saw or scythe sharpened by an expert, you have no idea what a difference it makes.

But we don't have to worry about all that now. We have chain saws, and except for their barbaric noise, they are one of the new tools a modern self-subsister selects with great joy.

When I write books praising windmills and hoes, someone always wants me to put in a good word for root cellars. I have nothing against root cellars. I used one extensively for several years. But it was already built (about 1920) and built right. To construct one like that now would cost more than two big freezers. For most families, a regular cellar can be used to store potatoes, onions, squash, and apples. For more perishable produce, a home freezer is the best answer to modern Subsistence.

People worry that if the electricity goes off for any length of time, their freezer full of meat would be ruined. Freezer companies usually have an insurance policy to cover the loss. We look at the prospect stoically. If the electricity goes off for any length of time, ruined food might be the least of our worries. In summer we could live off the garden and the live animals. In winter our deep freezer would remain effective because it sits in the unheated garage. In case of cataclysmic crisis, your home-made security would mean nothing anyway. You would have to share what you have with others because they would take it away from you if you didn't.

One of our neighbors makes excellent modern use of

an old dinner bell. In our neighborhood, there is lots of room for children to run and play, and, of course, they do. Because of all the shrubs and trees, visibility is about zero. When supper is ready, or homework time arrives, or bedtime, you can step out on the porch and bellow or lean on the car horn like most everyone does. Instead, this neighbor tolls her bell. You can hear it half a mile away, but it is a pleasant sound. Her children know that when that bell rings, it's time to go home.

We also know, by prearrangement, that a prolonged wild clanging means trouble. That idea follows a bygone custom on farms when a dinner bell ringing other than at mealtime meant fire. A dinner bell is faster than a telephone, especially where people spend lots of their time outdoors. Since no two old dinner bells sound exactly alike, it is quite possible to work up an excellent system of communication between outer-suburban homes. We are going to get one just as soon as we can find one we can afford. You can buy new inexpensive ones from places like Sears, Roebuck, & Company, but I'll try for an old one first.

Modern subsistence living must provide for the needs of the human spirit, not just the body. Otherwise, I might logically advocate living in caves and cooking over bonfires. Do not hesitate to spend your money on miracles of the electronic age, like stereo radios and tape recorders, and television. Modern FM stereo stations carry an excellent variety of faithfully reproduced music, and music is as necessary to the soul as strawberries and cream. Do not be fooled by the pseudo-intellectual view that television is a vast wasteland only. Watch a real war for a while. Or a politician getting his foot caught in his mouth. Television is the greatest thing that's happened to the education of the human race since the invention of books.

Speaking of books, start a library, if you haven't already. (Start it with this book and make us both happy.) Allow as many magazines as you can afford to come into your home. All kinds of magazines. Get your favorites bound into books to fatten your shelves. You will be preserving the very best history of our times.

Within a very few years, you will be able to buy videotapes of movies and plays and view them right through your television set. Then all the yearning you have felt to see famous Broadway stage plays will vanish. You will not have to endure New York; New York will come to Two Acre Eden.

New printing processes are bringing extremely faithful reproductions of art masterpieces within the reach of every pocketbook. The technology is already here. The problem is with artists, agents, and museums who for one financial reason or another like to keep things pretty much as they are. But in a short time, the concept of a building where people must go to see works of art will be obsolete. Instead, every Two Acre Eden will become an art museum and a shrine to human creativity.

Chapter 13

Suburban Wilderness: Daniel Boone, Where Are You?

I wish I knew who is responsible for perpetrating all the baloney about how dull, standardized, and inadequate life is in suburbia. I'm inclined to believe that the moviemakers and novelists don't actually *live* in the suburbs they describe so depreciatingly, but only sleep or attend cocktail parties there.

Maybe Montgomery County, Pennsylvania, 20 miles north of Philadelphia is different, but if it is, then there are a lot of "different" subdivisions around. We don't have much time for cocktail parties, and we sleep with one eye open, all in a jolly battle for survival with the wilderness of nature around us.

You think I exaggerate? Listen. For five years I was in mortal combat — and I mean that literally — with a Canadian goose, two raccoons, an opossum, and an assortment of other wild creatures you wouldn't believe.

It all seems incredible. If you drive the roads of that township, you will see mostly houses, factories, restaurants, shopping centers, and only rarely a farm. A blighted land, the wildlife lover might say, the tailbone

133

of creation. But all these trappings of modern civilization merely block your view of a land so wild it could lure Daniel Boone right out of his grave.

My first hint of this fact came shortly after we moved to our "tame" suburban home. I was disconsolately reading a letter from my brother, who was waxing eloquently about all his recent wildlife adventures far from this overcrowded eastern megalopolis. I nostalgically sorted out from memory the log cabin in southern Indiana where we had lived previously, our wild canoe trips on the lakes and rivers of Minnesota, the beloved farm in central Ohio where I grew to manhood.

My then four-year-old son stuck his head in the door. "There's a cow in the yard, Daddy," he said.

"Well, chase it out," I replied, deep in reverie.

"Okay."

A cow? I came to my senses and rushed outside. There, up at the other end of the lawn stood a buck deer, grazing on my crabgrass.

That old buck and I have had lots of fun in the intervening years. He's smart. He headquarters in that thimble-sized woods behind our yard because he knows no one would ever suspect any self-respecting deer would settle for such tame surroundings. We play hide-and-seek in that one-acre patch of brush. He allows me to come within 50 feet of him, no more. And if I bring unbelieving visitors back to meet him, he makes a liar out of me by not showing his crafty face. So I am left with only his tracks to prove his existence. Sometimes we get a glimpse of part of his harem thudding across the lawn, but the only time I see the whole resident herd of six deer is from the train I catch a mile away. They stand along the tracks just down from the station, as if to stick their tongues out at all us commuters who must spend our tawdry lives in the overcrowded city.

The first fall, I was spading up ground for my garden when suddenly I was transported to Minnesota or my native Killdeer Plains of Ohio. Overhead came the wavering, wild honking of Canadian geese winging southward—to me the most wonderful sound the wilderness ever produced. I was never really homesick after that.

But that was only the beginning. Within two miles of the house, right beside a factory, believe it or not, we found a beautiful pond on which a whole flock of Canadian geese wintered, not to mention an equal number of mallards and assorted other ducks. Many of these nest along the creek that flows among the houses in our valley.

In the spring, our family watched in breathless wonder while an aroused mother goose leaped from her nest to attack a horse and rider. The horse broke and ran, almost throwing its rider out of the saddle. Then with ugly hisses, mother goose turned on us, utterly changing my children's image of the nursery-rhyme writer of the same name.

One morning my wife came into the house complaining that the chickens had been dusting in her flower beds.

"Couldn't be," I countered. "The chickens haven't been out."

The mystery soon cleared up. Next morning, a whole flock of pheasants wandered into view while we ate breakfast. And they have continued to come. I trade them a fourth of my sweet corn for that pleasant morning parade. I think smugly about my brothers-in-law, who travel all the way from Kentucky to Wisconsin to hunt pheasants. From their accounts, I'm sure they could see more of them from our living room in one morning than they see in three days' hunting.

But any hunter who wishes to get his limit of rabbits can do it while mowing my lawn, and sometimes I wish someone would. One rabbit raises a family in the rock garden, another in the pachysandra next to the house, and another under the toolshed. If I didn't fence the vegetable garden and put protective shields around all the small trees, they'd reduce the place to a prairie in about three months.

We suffered a population explosion of squirrels two years ago. By late winter, things had reached the point where the poor squirrels were in danger of starvation and were systematically eating the buds off all the maple trees in the neighborhood. One neighboring gardener built a cage trap and caught 18 of them in 10 days—a fact my squirrel-hunting friends from Ohio refuse to believe.

One night we were awakened by the eeriest collection of growling and whining noises this side of a bobcat's den. On the patio we found the cat—our defender against things primeval—barring the door against a resolute raccoon, evidently lured by the good smells emanating from the kitchen. In the "good old days" of wilderness living, I'd seen a coon almost drown a dog, so I worried for the cat. We watched aghast, as neither coon nor cat showed any desire to retreat. Finally, the frontiersman (me) stepped into the fray. However, so soon from bed, I had forgotten one minor detail—shoes—and the coon understood this error in tactics immediately. Every time I wound up with the broom to deliver the coup de grace, the coon charged my big toe. You cannot swing a broom and hop around on one foot at the same time. Between my antics and the hysterical squeals of a wife and two kids, the coon finally became unnerved and retreated into the darkness.

Either he or his twin brother returned when the sweet corn ripened, and for a while it seemed we would have to do without fresh roasting ears. But so much did this coon love sweet corn that he forgot to go home one night, and the kids in the neighborhood treed him in the morning.

What do you do with a coon up a tree that you would like to keep out of your corn patch without taking drastic measures? Why, you capture him, of course, make a pet out of him, and teach him to eat something else. And who would climb the tree to take him captive? None other than the great white hunter who had been bragging about his wilderness prowess all these years.

Man may be king on the earth, but he draws no water up in a tree. A coon out on the end of a swaying branch has no fear of a human being staring him in the eyeball from a similar swaying branch. Coon crunched greedily whenever my weapon (my wife's broom) got close to him. Finally, he lost his footing for reasons I'll never know, since I was by that time hanging desperately onto mine. With many whoops and yells of barbarian gusto, the young audience of neighborhood savages below fell upon the hapless animal, wound him in the folds of burlap bags, and carried him triumphantly to a pen. Man had won again.

But by far the most bizarre encounter in my backyard jungle—indeed the only time I was actually wounded—was so unique in the annals of man against beast, even the doctor wouldn't believe it. I was raking grass clippings to use as mulch in the garden. I was barefooted, a folly I should have "been cured of" by then. Suddenly as I drew the rake toward me, I felt a sharp little sting. Looking down, I saw that I was being attacked by a wee, mouse-sized beast. I jumped straight into the air about two feet and the monster let go. He fell to the ground, rolled over, and came up charging me on his two hind feet like a microscopic grizzly bear. I had little time for such thoughts, but I yearned for a witness. That creature meant business, and I swung the rake as though I was going after a hole in one. Rake tines snapped off in various directions, and the monster, which we later identified as a short-tailed shrew, lay still.

Unfortunately, my wife is one of those girls who studied a little nursing in her misspent youth, and she immediately diagnosed rabies. I refused to go to the hospital; the bite had barely broken the skin. Wife called doctor, and you must understand that, especially when excited, she has a rich southern accent straight out of the Kentucky hills. According to her, the conversation went something like this:

"Mah husband's been bitten by a shrewww."

"A what?"

"A shrewww. Little bitty ole thing like a mouse."

Hesitation. Throat clearing. Slight gasp as if smothering a laugh.

"What's the matter," continues wife. "Didn't you-all ever hear of a shrewww bite?"

"Oh, of course. We have people coming in here every day wounded by shrews."

Both laugh. Lots of rapport over the telephone wires.

"He should wear gloves when handling such . . ."

"He didn't get bit on the hand, Doctor. On the foot."

"On the foot?"

"Yes, he didn't have his shoes on at the time."

"Oh." All rapport dwindles into suspicious silence.

"Could he get rabies, doctor?"

"Rabies? Well—uh—well, under the —uh—circumstances, don't you think he should come in and let me look at his—uh—foot?"

Then she really capped it off beautifully. "Ah'll try to persuade him, but you-all ought to know, he doesn't take much to doctors."

One would think that by now the law of survival would be uppermost in my mind and that I would remain boy scout prepared. But just the other morning, I lapsed into reverie that could have cost me another embarrassing exchange with the doctor. I was gathering eggs from our 12 hens. I reached into the bucket-turned-sideways-to-make-a-nest without first looking inside. My hand pawed something furry. With the instincts of a trapper, I jerked back. Bending over and peering into the nest, I came nose to nose with a big, fat opossum just finishing off my breakfast eggs.

I could also go into my battle with a local groundhog and a great horned owl, but I fear I have already stretched credibility to the breaking point.

Our local wildlife is not limited to animals. For birdwatching and wild flower hunting, I'll put my one-mile hike from Eden through the valley to the Reading rails up against almost any wild area of equal size. On any given day in spring or fall, I can spot 25 different species of birds without working at it. And in a little ravine next to the railroad track, we found 9 different kinds of wild flowers in a radius of 25 feet. Through that ravine ripples a stream that drains through several subdivisions. The water is pure and full of several kinds of minnows.

Unlike more rural farm areas I know, not much chemical spraying of weeds is done by our township. We are therefore treated throughout the growing season to wild strawberries, raspberries, blackberries, elderberries, wineberries, and a wonderful assortment of wild crab apples and thorn apples. And there are plenty of persimmons, hickory nuts, and walnuts, too.

What I am trying to say, really, is that man and the wild things he loves need not be mutually exclusive. They can live together. Farms, factories, shopping centers, and housing developments can exist beside each other, using the good land without ruining it. All it takes is common sense overcoming greed, and the desire for more quality of life, not mere quantity of experiences.

The other day I found a flint arrowhead in the garden. I showed it to my son and explained something about Indians to him. Bug-eyed, he looked toward the woods and asked me how the arrowhead got in our garden. I told him the Indians roamed this land many years ago, but were gone now. He only half believed me.

Chapter 14

What Do You Do Out There All the Time?

One August day when the kids were whining out of sheer boredom, I made them each a butterfly net: a broom handle affixed to a wire loop on which my wife sewed a net of old window curtain. The children were soon having so much fun, I made a net for myself. Chasing a choice zebra swallowtail madly down the road ditch, I happened to catch sight of a neighbor leaning on his fence, watching me with a most peculiar look on his face. I stopped.

"Hi," I said. I felt I should defend myself some way. "That's a pretty rare butterfly, you know." Followed by my best sheepish grin.

He just stared and shook his head.

Oh well. Maybe the knack of enjoying yourself in the country is a gift one is born with, like throwing a good knuckleball, and cannot be learned. I've about arrived at that conclusion after hearing for the 548th time the question, "But what do you *do* out there all the time?"

Behind that question lies a one-eyed view of the world. The urbanite assumes that out in the country, one suffers from a lack of Culture: no theaters, no large libraries, no opera, no Philharmonic, no great museums, arboretums, observatories; no famous restaurants where the great and near-great meet; no Saks Fifth Avenue, no haute couture, not even the *New York Times* in the morning. My God, how can you *survive?*

Even if the countryman were cut off from these sources of high refinement (which of course he isn't, what with stereo, TV, books, magazines, and movies; he can't escape "culture" if he wanted to), I don't think his education would suffer as much as the urbanite's, whose experiences are limited to the big city and who is by far, more cut off from the country than the ruralist is from the city. Provincial, in my opinion, has become a term that fits the center-city dweller.

Great cultural centers are found in the cities because only there do enough people live to support them. But I wonder if it doesn't go deeper than that. Perhaps in the city the environment is so artificial that people need, psychologically, walls upon which to hang the beauty that the countryman sees around him every day.

But that is only one aspect of culture anyway. In the true meaning of the word, there is more American culture alive and healthy in Sleepy Eye, Minnesota, or Damp Hollow, Kentucky, than there is in the whole of New York's Metropolitan Museum of Art. The countryside is one vast human library of twice-told history, traditional music, and oral literature. As every important novelist has discovered — picturesque language, drama, conflict — the guts of great literature do not come out of a writer's head. They exist, are now happening, wherever human beings get together. All the writer has to do is watch, listen, and have the brains to recognize the gems that drop from the lips of his neighbors.

Indeed, Folklore, or the collecting of it, is one of my favorite pastimes in the country. I like to think that I'm something of a professional folklorist—another of those nonpaying occupations I've picked up along the way. I interview people (that is, I chew the fat with them) and

141

"collect" their folk tales, traditional stories, old jokes, superstitions, folk songs, historical reminiscences, ghost stories, weather lore, and traditional work methods. I look for folk artists, craftsmen, and people with a reputation as folk singers or storytellers. Back at my desk, I transcribe the notes or tapes, annotate my collection with sources of similar lore collected in other regions, and I have bound my typewritten collection into a "book." I think I've learned more about America this way than I ever did from history books.

Here are some examples of quaint folklore I recorded in a county in Ohio. These stories are told and retold, and the first one, about a man who lived in the early 1800s, has been handed down from one generation to the next for a century with little change.

Bowsher couldn't read nor write, but that didn't stop him. He had a grocery and kept people's accounts with pictures. When you owed him for something, he would draw the thing you got on a board or a shingle or a piece of paper. Like if you bought an ax, he'd take down the shingle that he'd drawn your likeness on, and draw an ax under it. Once a man owed him for a long time, so when he came into the store, Bowsher got down this man's "account," so they could settle up. The first drawing was a pitchfork, they could both tell that easy enough. The next drawing was just a round circle. Bowsher said it was a cheese. The customer said, "No, tain't. We don't eat cheese. I never bought no cheese off you." They went round and round over it, raising up a pretty good storm. But then Bowsher remembered. "By God, I know. It's a grindstone. I forgot to put the hole in it." The other man then did recollect that he'd bought a grindstone, so he paid up.

There was this big shot came into the county looking for some land to buy with a barn on it. He told our real estate dealer what he wanted, and the dealer said, yes, he had some places like that. So they drove out to look at some. The dealer began to tell the man about several places, so he'd get a better idea of what the big shot was looking for. But this wiseacre told the dealer never to mind with his questions and sales talk. He had two eyes to see with and he'd know whether he was going to buy when he saw it. Wasn't no use trying to give *him* a sell. So the dealer thought to himself, okay, big shot, we'll take care of *you*. He had a place for sale that had a barn on it, okay? The barn even had a cement floor in it. Only trouble was, the whole back part of the roof had blown off—you could throw a cat through that roof almost anywheres. Well, they got there and the dealer walked into the barn first and sidled the big shot over under a haymow right fast. Then he talked floor. He talked floor until he was blue in the face and he never let the big shot get his mind off that pretty concrete. All the while, he kept backing the big shot under the haymow farther, talking floor. He sold the wiseacre a barn with no roof on it.

A rain came up fast and Carl was plowing. He wanted awful bad to get the field finished before the storm hit, so he was pushing that old lug-wheeled tractor as fast as it would go. All of a sudden, the motor began to buck up and miss—probably dirt in the gas line. It would go a spell, then sputter, then go again. Sometimes stop altogether. Carl, one eye on the clouds, started to get mad and was calling the tractor some pretty desperate names. Pretty soon, he really blew his stack and grabbed a stick laying on the fencerow and smacked the tractor over the fender, hard. Wouldn't you know, the sputtering quit and the motor roared. So he climbs on and starts back across the field. Every time the motor started missing, he'd stand up and whale the daylights out of the fender with his stick. And the tractor always seemed to lurch on for a while. He beat that poor machine all the way across the field and back and finished before the rain hit.

I've collected nearly a book full of superstition and folk belief, some of it still practiced. I know of people who still think stump water is healthful (how do you know it's not?), that a bird banging against a window foretells death, that a sun dog is a sign of stormy weather (it is), and that a roof must be laid in the dark of the moon or the shingles will curl up and come off. Why do such beliefs continue in tradition? As an old farmer told me confidentially one time: "You know, I don't really believe in religion, but I keep going to church because I might be wrong."

As I travel around the countryside collecting stories, I watch for native art: for example, a good self-trained or untrained painter far from the influence of New York or Paris and the very calculated pseudo-freedom of university art schools. It is amazing how often, in very small villages, I will walk into a restaurant and find the walls decorated with the paintings of a local artist. The art is not necessarily good (whatever that means), but it is always interesting. One of these days, someone is going to be smart enough to do a book out of it: *Cafe Art along Highway 66*.

Since a folk artist by definition is untrained or self-trained, I've tried to become one myself. The same sort of material that Van Gogh, Millet, and Wyeth turned into masterpieces is part of my environment every day, I figured. Why not paint my countryside? At the rate population is growing, I might be recording a vanishing scene.

So last winter, I declared to the family that I intended to turn out a few canvases. For Christmas my wife gave me a set of oils, instructions, brushes — the whole works. I spread the tools of my newly acquired trade over the kitchen table. In my mind was this glorious color slide I had taken of a stalk of corn in the snow — the idea copied from a Wyeth painting. But as I began to put paint to canvas, I did not consult the photo. Only slobs painted from photos, someone had told me.

What Do You Do Out There All the Time?

I slaved away. Rather, I should say *we* slaved away. Both son and daughter had spread watercolors and paper on either side of me, ready to learn from the master. Had Daddy ever painted a picture before? Could Daddy paint as good as Andrew Wyeth? Could they use Daddy's oils and canvas too? Carol joined the party at the other end of the table and began one of those paint-by-numbers pictures while I was lecturing the children to rely on their own creativity.

Within hours, the kids had produced 14 paintings each, and taped them to the walls, the refrigerator, and the bedroom doors. I was still trying to figure out how to paint snow. How *do* you paint white snow on a white canvas, anyhow? My feeble attempts were met with silence by my young audience, while every dab Carol placed in her confounded numbered diagram brought sighs of wonder and appreciation from them. Creativity was taking a beating, but some of those young attempts hanging on the refrigerator were certainly fine examples of primitive art. For two weeks the place looked like an art museum, and in the end, Carol's project was declared the first-place winner by a vote of 3 to 1.

The wonderful thing about your own creations is the way your family treasures them. I have a painting of my son done by my sister that I wouldn't trade for a genuine Van Gogh. Nor the painting daughter Jenny did for me for Father's Day. When I did a crayon drawing of a fox for my son, he hung it on his bedroom door and wouldn't allow anyone to take it down for a year, however awful it seemed to the rest of us. I just know that the secret of all successful artistic creation is love.

Since brushes are definitely not my bag, I've gone to a camera to conjure up my "art." Right on my lawn there are lots of things that haven't been photographed artistically. I know of only one photo of a firefly at its blazing moment of glory. When's the last time you've seen a color shot of a newly emerging cone on a tamarack tree — purple against the new green needles? I have been unable to find many good, published color slides of wild American fungi.

Two Acre Eden

How about a movie: *The Life and Death of a Potato Bug?*
And a camera is the only way I know to "collect" interesting
barns, houses, sheds, and fences.

I try to keep a record — both on film and in notebook
— of all the plants, bugs, and animals that cross my two
acres. It's amazing how much "world" is contained on so
small a plot of ground.

Everybody knows about bird-watching these days,
and we bird-watchers aren't looked upon as oddities anymore. But I have always wondered why we have only bird-
watchers. An equally enjoyable hobby is bug-watching: the
variety is greater, the watching is generally easier, and
bugs are as beautiful as birds.

I make a hobby out of watching, period. Observing
a den of young groundhogs beats most of the programs
on television. Fox-watching isn't as interesting as girl-
watching, but it demands more skill. Ant-watching is an
absolutely fascinating study in sociology.

In fact, the only kind of watching that doesn't fit
the countryside is watch-watching. On Two Acre Eden limit
yourself to one clock and hang it in the top of a big tree
where no one can see it.

Most country pastimes have to do with hunting
things. I think the countryman has never really come out
of what the anthropologists call the Hunting and Gathering
Stage in human civilization. At least we haven't. The only
difference is that we hunt not out of dire need as the
cavemen did, but more for the fun of it.

One thing we hunt most avidly is the mushroom.
Time was when hunting mushrooms was even kookier than
watching birds. It's actually exciting to go after mushrooms,
especially morels. They are hard to see, for one thing. I
can't really explain the thrill of it. You just have to get
the swing of it by experience.

Put a tribe of Logsdons in the woods hunting morels
in the first week of May, and you'll have no trouble keeping
track of them. First of all, there are so many of us: grand-
parents, parents, teenagers, on down to toddling babies.
From the latter comes a continuous whine of "can't get

over the fence," or, "can't find Mommy." Then Mommy becomes very "findable" because she is screaming hysterically: "I found one, I found one!" as if she were talking about ten-dollar bills. Soon Grandfather is roaring from way down the other end of the woods for everyone to "come quick!" We all know this means he has hit the mother lode, a big patch of morels. Everyone begins running toward the sound of Grandfather's voice. Small children wail in abandonment. No one cares. Mushroom fever is on us. We converge on Grandfather from all directions and pounce from one morel to another, while he stands there and grins. Sometimes two of us see the same mushroom at the same time. We collide on our way to pick it. We scramble for every morel: the person who finds the most will lord it over the others for weeks.

Finally the last of the mushrooms is picked. Immediately and always, a great argument issues from a score of throats over the shortest way back to the cars. Grandfather wins because he can still outshout everyone. Most of the in-laws follow him. Brother, sisters, and I shake our heads sadly and go our own way. We know that Grandfather is almost always wrong. We collect the abandoned children and beat him back to the car by 15 minutes.

Morel hunting has become so popular that some locales in Michigan put out brochures and reports for the benefit of out-of-state hunters. Iowa, Ohio, and Indiana newspapers faithfully report the biggest morel of the season, and farmers who want to save their woodlots for their own hunting, have to post the property and patrol it, or be overrun by eager hunters from town.

The morel, also called sponge mushroom or honeycomb, because that's what it looks like, is easy to identify and tastes as good as truffles. You can easily identify the common kind, but you will pass up some perfectly good morels that don't look quite like the prototype in the books. There is a very small morel that grows earliest in spring and is found only by the best hunters, who call it the "leaf mushroom" (accent the second syllable of mushroom). There is a morel that I have found only under old pear trees; another grows along railroad tracks. The one that grows under elm trees has a different texture than the one that grows under pin oak trees. There's a long-stemmed kind that most people would pass up for a toadstool. And there is the false morel which contains a psychedelic drug and is not safe to eat. It may or may not make you feel like you've just downed two martinis.

There is only one law in mushroom hunting. Do not try to be guided by illustrations in a book. Take some old hunter along with you who *knows*. You know that he knows because he is still alive.

We are hooked on country auctions because we are hooked on Hunting and Gathering second-rate antiques (junk). But the money we waste is our very own, and we rationalize by saying that our treasures may someday become valuable. And in the meantime we can pick up a perfectly good set of furniture cheap.

Farm sales aren't half the fun they were when Grandmother was alive. Even after we, her children (we got in the habit of calling her Grandmother after the third generation began to arrive), had started our own families and gone our own ways, Grandmother would keep a sharp eye on the papers and let us all know when one of those really good farm sales (the ones advertising lots of antiques and other items "too numerous to mention") was going to occur deep in her Ohio country. Then my wife and I would pack up the kids and head for home. Arriving there, we'd find the barnyard already full of cars belonging to other family members equally affected by auction fever.

We'd barely have time to eat before the whole caravan shoved off, Grandmother in the lead. She dispensed the history of every farm we passed to anyone fortunate (or unfortunate) enough to be riding in her car. Eventually we would end up on a lonely gravel road, cornstalks high on either side, that would lead finally to an old farm with cars parked two football fields long in each direction along the road ditch.

Part of the game for Grandmother was to arrive late like this, when all the good parking spaces were taken, and then nose her station wagon haughtily up to the very yard of the farmhouse and park the car where she darn well pleased. She would simply stare right through anybody who was trying to direct traffic away from the center of activity. She got away with it every time.

The rest of our caravan would park meekly down the road, which meant that by the time we walked up to the house, Grandmother had already pawed through all the household goods, switching items around in those boxes of "miscellaneous" until she had everything she wanted in one box and wouldn't have to bid on all the others. She would not let us make any "discoveries" on our own; she'd been all through it already and would guide us furtively from one goody to another. "Here's a really *old* rolling pin," she'd whisper to me. "I'm gonna get that for Carol." That was her joke. She eventually bought all her married daughters and daughters-in-law a rolling pin "to whack your husbands with."

She liked to pretend she was an expert dealer in antiques. She'd pick up a piece of pottery that other people were admiring, wave it dramatically at one of her offspring three tables away and pontificate loudly: "Pure trash." But when she spotted something she wanted to buy, she would try to throw the crowd off by lying in a loud, earnest whisper: "Don't waste your time bidding on that, Gene. That's Sears, Roebuck & Company, circa 1944."

She attended auctions like a CIA agent visiting Hong Kong. Suddenly, I'd feel an elbow in my ribs. Grandmother would be standing there, muttering through clenched teeth. "Don't look now, but under that card table over by that lilac bush there's a box we've got to get. There's a *McGuffey's Reader* in the bottom of it. I piled a whole bunch of *Reader's Digest* Condensed Books on top of it." Or again: "Saunter slowly over to the barn and take a look in the third horse manger from the back. Set of horse hames in there and I think the metal is brass. If it is, throw them under that pile of junk outside the barn door, and we'll get the whole shootin' match for a dollar."

When the auction started, she was always right up

there, nose to nose with the auctioneer. She could elbow her way through a crowd of porcupines. Over the years she equipped about four houses with furniture that would have cost four daughters hundreds of dollars in stores, but cost her only $67.50. She knew when to bid and when to go home. She could wait unflinchingly in 90-degree heat, or zero cold, or drizzling rain for that one moment when the auctioneer got tired or impatient and gaveled off five sturdy matching chairs for 50¢. She never paid more than five dollars for anything, but put together a fairly substantial collection of antique pottery. Her procedure in buying country antiques was simple: "I don't really care how old a thing is, or how rare. I can't afford that good stuff anyway. I try to buy what I think is beautiful. If I'm right, it will someday become valuable. If I'm wrong, I've still got my money's worth out of it in enjoyment."

Farm auctions are also good places to save money on garden tools, fencing, lumber, posts, siding, wire, bolts, carpentry tools, scythes, chicken waterers, and much more. All of this stuff may very well be necessary for your little farm. At sales you may get it reasonably, if you are patient. Auctions involve a lot of standing around and waiting—a good time to collect folklore.

Another hunting and gathering project in the country is searching for Indian artifacts in cornfields. Arrowheads can be found on bare winter and early spring fields in most parts of the country, and farmers have made an exciting hobby of finding and collecting them for years. Those who don't collect Indian relics themselves will generally allow you to plod their fields in early spring before planting time. That is the best time to hunt, because winter rains have by then washed into view the maximum number of relics. After the land is plowed again, you can't find much until more rains have washed the loose dirt away from stones imbedded in it.

Keep your eyes open in your garden too. I found two arrowheads and a clay pipe bowl in mine last spring. In the fall, we stroll along stream banks where the water has washed up piles of stone and gravel. A sharp eye can sometimes spot relics there.

Generally I have the best luck roving in corn-stubble fields above a stream or river. These are likely spots for former Indian campsites. If I begin to see tiny flint shavings on the ground, I know I'm on the right track because flint is not native to most areas and had to be brought in by Indians. A good number of chips means Indians were once busy on the spot making arrowheads.

Of course, hunting Indian relics is only one kind of "rock hounding." No matter where you live in the country, a few hikes can be the start of a rock collection.

A few summers ago, my brother-in-law and I decided, quite disastrously as it turned out, really to get into the Indian relic business in earnest. "Why not," he suggested about two o'clock one morning, "dig up an Indian mound with a backhoe?"

"Why not," I echoed dramatically.

I'll tell you why not. (1) In one fell swoop, you can ruin an archaeological site for all future study. (2) Digging up an Indian mound correctly (or even incorrectly) requires at least a year and the help of a small army.

We rationalized that by the skin of our teeth, we might actually qualify on both counts. Hadn't I minored in anthropology in grad school? Didn't brother-in-law know how to run a backhoe? Well, he knew as much about back-hoes as I did about Indian mounds, by hickory. And getting together a small army was no trouble. The Logsdon clan rides again.

And so it came to pass that one beautiful day in July, we began to dig holes in a hillside. On hand were all the members of the family clan who could walk, from the first to the third generation. In the eyes of each danced visions of smooth shale bannerstones, ceremonial amulets, silver beads, copper spearheads, flint scrapers, clay pots decorated with red ocher—all the treasures that other people had found in other mounds.

Ever since I could remember, this particular hill that we planned to excavate had been pointed out to me as an

Indian mound — so long that I had finally believed it. It did stand alone in a valley by a stream without any particular excuse for being where it was unless man had put it there. It had a peculiar shape to it, pear shaped with a certain flatness to the top of it, just as the book said some mounds were built.

Brother-in-law wheeled the backhoe up against the flank of the hill. Our original idea was to dig a narrow trench through the mound as deep as we could go. Then when we struck a midden, or a stone tomb, or a pile of silver amulets, or a mass grave of skeletons, we'd stop and proceed to excavate our treasures with trowels and toothbrushes in the best archaeological style.

The trouble with this plan was that it was hatched over several cans of beer a few miles distant from the mound, not on the site. The hill was quite large, you see, and, of course, we actually *knew* it was large, having spent half our childhood playing on it. But not until we had the backhoe out there did we really understand how much dirt we were up against. You could bury 25 backhoes in that hill and still have room for a dozen bulldozers.

Undaunted, we decided to dig our trench into the innards of the hill just as far as we could. Surely by then we'd strike the rock-covered inner chamber we were sure was under the dirt. Brother-in-law roared into action. He *did* know as much about backhoes as I did about mounds, by golly. It only took him an hour to figure out which levers controlled which movements of the machine. In only an hour he had a hole dug nearly deep enough to bury a cat in.

But by afternoon, a fairly respectable trench gaped out of the slope of the hill. At first we saved every rock and pebble the backhoe unearthed, as each member of the tribe worried and sifted through the dirt piled along the trench. Every 15 minutes we'd all pile into the trench and study the layers of soil with fervent professionalism, as if we knew exactly what we were doing. Every microscopic black particle was immediately labeled charcoal from an ancient fire; any lump of clay even faintly red in color, was deduced to be ocher; any speck of white crumbling limestone brought on an earnest geological debate over "Stones Native to This Country."

Along about dark, eureka! A bone protruded from the side of the trench. A bone. A bone! The shout aroused the whole camp, and 18 old and young one-day veterans of archaeology dove into the trench.

"A fibia," I said solemnly.

"Don't touch it. It might break," said sister Marilyn.

"I think you mean tibia," first brother-in-law remarked.

"Holy smokes, there's *more* bones behind this one," shouts third brother-in-law. He is scraping at the clay wall with abandon.

I remembered that Carol in her first-year nursing had to memorize all the human bones. "Carol, get over here quick. It's a backbone, it is, by damn, it is."

We waited breathlessly for Carol to give a professional identification. We helped her along.

"Femur."

"Vertebrae."

"Tibia."

"Fibula."

"Metatarsal."

"I can't tell," says Carol. "You got to get it out farther."

From above the trench, Grandfather arrived from the shade of a tree he'd been sitting under, took one look and roared. "Backbone? It sure is. Right off an old dead sheep!"

We dug for two days and filled in the trench for another, and we did not find so much as a piece of flint or the hair of an Indian's eyebrow. Not only that, but sometime during the excitement of the first day, I filled the oil chamber on the tractor motor with hydraulic oil instead of motor oil, and just a mile before we got the backhoe back to its rightful owner, she threw a rod and died.

There must be a moral in this somewhere, but all I can say is that we do have fun in the country, though we're running short on friends.

Two Acre Eden

Rooting around in junk piles can be fun. What you are looking for is old glass. In a really old junk heap, the tin and cheaper forms of pottery have rotted away, and most of the steel. But glass remains, and if you are lucky, you can find old pieces that have not been broken — especially old bottles. And, of course, antiquers are all going nuts over old bottles.

Another good place to find bottles is in barns. Great-grandad used to have to hide his whiskey from Great-grandmother, and he usually stuck the bottles in nooks and crannies among the beams and rafters of the barn. He also used old bottles to hold the medicines he administered to sick animals, and you might find some of them stashed away in the barn, too.

Barns are delightful places anyway; just to stand in one and listen to the pigeons, or watch the moon come up behind it. We should preserve a few old barns with hay in them for children to jump in. And with the hay rope pulled down to make a swing, so kids can glide back and forth the full length of the barn on rainy days, like we used to do.

Today we must spend a lot of money developing recreation centers for children. Not all progress is forward.

In every old barn there is some treasure (unless I have visited it before you). Not something worth much money, but some old tool, some well-carved handle, some old bit of horse harness, something out of the past that you can hang in your house and cherish forever. If you have an old barn on your Two Acre Eden, love it. Be good to it. Put animals in it again. Take a stab at using those old forks and shovels and grain buckets. There is an infinite peace about it. Not all progress is forward.

Time was, when I would have made a big deal here out of hunting and fishing, archery and shooting. These sports are loved by many countrymen, and I have avidly participated.

But the older I get, the less prone I am to shoot anything. And I am least prone to encourage others. True, wild game must be "harvested" just like domestic animals.

What Do You Do Out There All the Time?

Most wild animals have a tendency to overpopulate — especially deer and woodchucks — to the point where they become pests or starve each other out. But most humans have a tendency to overkill, and I've seen more of that than I can take.

If you need meat, bagging a deer or pheasant does nature a favor in a way. There aren't enough wolves and cougars and wildcats to keep down the deer population, and when there are too many deer, they can starve to death in the winter. Pheasant populations rise and fall regardless of hunting, say the wildlife people. It is mostly illegal to kill hen pheasants though, and I hope fervently that you get caught if you do it. Squirrels can overpopulate too, as I found out. If you have some woods a safe distance from houses, teach your son how to handle a .22 rifle and let him bag a few squirrels every fall.

I don't really hold with all this talk about guns teaching violence. I was brought up around guns, and was a crack shot at 12 — a lot cracker than I am today. What I learned was respect for life. Once I disobeyed my father and shot a nongame bird — a turtledove. He had taught me the songbird list — all the birds that were not to be shot. He scolded me severely and relieved me of my rifle for a month. He said he'd heard that a turtledove would return to the spot where its mate was killed and sing its mournful song until it died of a broken heart.

And you know another turtledove *did* sit there on the telephone wire where I had slain the first one, and cooed away mournfully for several days. I was so ashamed that I cried. And never shot any birds except sparrows and starlings again.

The only times I really enjoy bagging game or hooking fish are on our family "survival" games, which are as close as we come to having a family reunion. The idea is for the whole tribe to retreat to the woods along the river with rifles, knives, fishing poles, nets, salt, butter, and lots of enthusiasm. The challenge is to grub up enough food from the land and waters to keep from starving from 6:00

A.M. to 10:00 P.M. The rules prohibit eating a big breakfast beforehand.

We divide into groups, each responsible for a particular course of our wilderness meal: salad, meat, fish, vegetables, dessert. We've all read Euell Gibbons' *Stalking the Wild Asparagus* (New York: McKay, 1970) and other books on wild food, and consider ourselves experts in survival.

By noon, enthusiasm has been replaced by hunger. The fish won't bite, and the squirrels won't show. The dessert department has picked two quarts of blackberries and eaten them all on the way back to camp. Grandfather has netted half a bucket of crayfish, the tails of which, boiled in water, will taste like lobster, but are so small each of us knows he can eat the whole mess himself. The vegetable gang has found a stand of wood lilies, but can't remember exactly which part Mr. Gibbons said was good to eat. I find enough cattail roots for three people.

By 6:00 P.M., we have garnered 14 dandelion roots, 2 infant bluegills, a young groundhog (which earlier everyone swore they would not eat, but now, panged by hunger, we decide to try after all), 5 more quarts of blackberries, the crayfish tails, the cattail roots, and an assortment of weed leaves, of which only the sourgrass and purslane we know to be fairly tasty. We concoct a tea from sassafras roots.

Once cooked, the whole business disappears down 18 throats in five minutes. We rave about how tasty everything is. We eye the nearby cornfield.

"Oh no, that's not fair," Grandfather remonstrates. "You can't eat corn, that's not wild. Besides that would be stealing."

"It's not immoral to steal food when you are starving to death," someone says solemnly.

In a trice, off come 18 ears of corn. It is field corn, but we are so hungry it tastes like fine roasting ears. We decide to pay the farmer for our theft.

The day of survival ends. The party breaks up. We put out the fire. It has been another memorable day. Even the children didn't cry too much. And they certainly learned the meaning of survival and the blessedness of civilization. *These* kids aren't going to grow up thinking nature is a loving mother. We all go home and strip the refrigerators bare.

If you have space and you fancy tennis, why not build a tennis court? A clay court need not be terribly expensive, if you have the right kind of clay. You don't *have* to have a high regulation backstop. Build a lower one with chicken wire. Some clever people know how to get old telephone poles from the telephone company for a frame. If you have a grove of your own cedar trees that are too crowded, you can get good poles there too. If you have an old barn, you may have one ready-made backstop.

If you have sports-minded youngsters and a fairly level pasture, they will eventually talk you into letting them shape up a baseball diamond.

If you have hills, you will have sleds and toboggans.

If you have a pond, you will have ice skates. If you put a pole light up at the pond, you will have hockey and lots of young acquaintances to keep you in touch and never allow a generation gap to develop.

If you have snow, you will be tempted to have a snowmobile. If you give in to temptation, I hope you don't live near me. Snowmobiles are a lot of fun but are monstrously noisy. No winter wilderness is safe from their depredations. And those types who care nothing about the wilderness and are too lazy to hike the winter stillness anyway now have access to almost everywhere. They scare away wildlife, knock over little trees, pollute, and destroy. I feel the same about motorcycles, motorboats, helicopters, dune buggies, go-carts, and swamp buggies. Fortunately, stricter laws on their use and stringent regulations on mufflers are easing the problems.

Another pastime we've found to be most gratifying over the years is visiting cemeteries. The older, the better. I know of any number of very small, untended graveyards in pasture corners or the wood's edge on an abandoned farm. Sometimes the stones themselves are of interest; some designs and stonework are examples of truly native

American art. Or you can collect epitaphs. Or religious symbols. Or look for your ancestors. Or check out a country's history. Or simply enjoy the well-groomed grass, trees, and bushes usually found there. It is somehow odd that we often take better care of the homes of our dead bodies than those of our live bodies.

Chapter 15

How *Not* to Do
Almost Anything

I am an expert in the nonconstruction of sheds, stone walls, fences, ponds, sidewalks, outdoor fireplaces, gates, log cabins, boats — almost anything. I am an authority on the Wrong Way, so I can bring you greater wisdom.

Not that I mind my mistakes; I revel in them. Anyone can follow instructions. Only mavericks who stray from beaten paths discover the unknown. If my wayward efforts result in no ovations, what is that to me? The excitement of life is in the act of attaining, not the attainment.

At age nine, I embarked on my first engineering venture: building a raft. Of course, at the time my sister and I would have told you we were building a Viking warship for a long voyage of discovery and conquest. While we hammered nails into boards and posts we had scrounged off the woodpiles behind the barn, we argued about whether to christen our ship *Moby Dick* or *Rumrunner.* More thought went into the debate than into the construction, and it was afternoon before our ocean liner was finished. We dragged it to the creek and set sail for Newfoundland. The raft immediately sank. I jumped to shore. The raft rose with Sis. It was quite obvious that only one of us could go to Newfoundland at a time.

So began the pattern of my life: an overwhelming desire to make things, unaccompanied either by the discipline to follow directions or the means to get the right equipment and material for the job. As a result I have left a trail of brilliantly contrived near-successes. My picture frames are always just a little crooked, my doors barely stick, my sidewalks almost do not crack, my shelves sag only a wee bit. And everything I have made will self-destruct within two months after I die.

I was bound to have a barn. But to build one properly of the size I wanted would have cost me a minimum of $600. In pioneer times, whole homesteads were built for less than that.

I remember that in my boyhood, farmers made an extremely cheap shelter for hogs by heaping a strawstack over a big frame of poles. I didn't have any straw, but lots of grass clippings. Why wouldn't they work? And my barn would look as though it had a thatched roof. Perhaps. I love thatched roofs.

To the woods I went for poles to frame my "barn." Oak and cedar make good posts, so I cut ash. I had lots of ash the right size. I dug holes with the post-hole digger at each corner of my thatched dream and two more along each long wall; tramped in the posts; nailed old two by sixes around the top connecting them all, which formed a sort of roofline. Over this I laid the branches left over from the ash trees, then started heaping on my grass thatch.

Merrily, I nailed on some used siding (begged from a friend). I ran out of siding, so I left the side facing southeast open, away from the weather, with only a chicken-wire fence across it. In winter I could put corn shocks along the fencing to keep the chickens snug inside. The barn was shaping up. It looked like a cross between a Scottish crofter's sheep shed and a blind Bantu's jungle hut.

Then it rained. The water went right through my thatched roof. I piled on more old hay. Still just a sieve. Grandfather could shape a haystack that shed water like a tin roof, but the rain dribbled right through mine. More hay. More rain. The roof collapsed.

So I removed the hay. It made excellent mulch. Bowing somewhat to convention, I built a regular shingled roof. But how steep do you pitch a roof? I decided the steeper, the better.

My barn was beginning to look almost respectable. To me. And I had spent only $60 so far. The neighbors were a little nervous. One of the more narrow-minded asked me if I had obtained a building permit—a little detail I had somehow overlooked. I inquired at the proper office, found I had to draw a rough map of my property and show exactly where the building I proposed to build would stand. (I did not think I should trouble them with the fact that the shed was already built.) Just by luck, my barn stood far enough from my property boundaries to comply with the zoning ordinance. I received my permit. Five dollars please.

My father-in-law, a farmer and master builder, came to visit us. He took one look at my barn and doubled over with laughter. "The first strong wind that comes through here will blow that roof clean into the middle of next week," he chortled. "It's too steep. It stands up too straight against the wind."

I pondered that statement for a week. Maybe he was right. So I invented a new device in architectural engineering, which I call the "Hurricane Inhibitor." It's just a long two by four, nailed to the bottom of one wall of the shed inside and to the roof rafter on the opposite side. Several of these staggered through the building do not make for easy walking, but if the wind blows hard enough to blast the roof into the middle of next week, it will have to take the whole building along.

The final blow to my ego came when the tax man came around to appraise my "new" building. He walked on up the long path to the shed while we waited fearfully in the house for his verdict. It didn't take him very long. He returned, looked at me with great pity, and shook his head. "I'm afraid I can't morally put any value on that—

thing. "It's, it's . . ." he groped for words, found none, shrugged. I tried very hard to view the situation soberly. He drove away, still shaking his head.

I've never come up against a stone wall I couldn't somehow identify with. To think that the rocks that make them possible lie free for the taking in unlimited numbers over the crust of the earth appeals to my sense of thriftiness. To build a dry stone wall seems to me the highest of human endeavors: creating useful art out of a pile of rocks everyone wants to get rid of. I had to try my hand at it.

Immediately after we bought Two Acre Eden, we began collecting rocks. But we never could stockpile enough for a wall. Rocks are so handy. We built a terraced flower garden with them. We used them for borders and walks. Smaller ones were thrown in fury at dogs loping through the vegetables.

We used up all our own rocks, then began hauling some home in the trunk of the car. We had a crazy idea of collecting one rock from every state to put in the rock garden. I carried one home from Wisconsin in my suitcase on the plane once. I remember when I asked my neighbor, Fred, if he had any rocks he didn't want. He gazed at the skies and almost wept. He pointed at his garden, which was literally covered with them. "Those are too little," I said. "Not as small as the ones in your head," he replied.

We could find plenty of rocks around, but the job of transporting them to our property in sufficient numbers became nearly impossible. It seemed ridiculous to turn to the stone quarry, but that we did.

At least, at the quarry, the people didn't think we were crazy. In fact they saved the best flat, square-cornered rocks they blasted out of the ground for idiots like me who wanted to build stone walls. But these nice rock slabs were three times more expensive than the plain old lopsided variety. I said I'd take the lopsided ones. He warned me that hardly anyone tried to build walls out of them. I remained adamant. How many did I want? I couldn't answer that intelligently. How big is the wall you intend to build? I didn't know that either. Rapidly I multiplied dollars times tons. I'll take three tons, I said bravely. Three tons sounded like a small mountain's worth.

A couple of days later a big truck groaned into the driveway and up to the barn, trampling everything in its path. Up went the bed, and out dribbled three tons. It looked like about three wheelbarrow loads.

But it was a start. I went to work like a kid with building blocks. In my mind was this fabulous vision of dry stone walls, laid straight and strong without mortar, like the ones I had seen in Maine. The blood of pioneers coursed in my veins. Mortar was beneath my dignity. I laid rocks. In about ten minutes, I realized that a dry wall has to be at least two feet wide, just as the blasted book said. You are supposed to dig a ditch about two feet deep, putting the biggest boulders into it first. Then you lay two runs of the squarer rocks alongside each other, and drop the little rounder rocks in the middle, always keeping the two outer runs slanting *in*ward. Mine refused to slant inward. In fact, the only things that would slant inward were the vertebrae in my back.

The awful, absolute truth staring me in my sweat-soaked brow was that a wall of this thickness was going to take enough rocks to make stock jump 30 points in the stone-quarry business.

I jumped in the car and got some sand and mortar. Heck, it wouldn't take much to stick those rocks together. Six sacks of sand and two of mortar and home.

The next weekend, I was organized to build a wall: Pile of sand, sack of mortar, water, hoe to stir it up, trowel, two children in eager anticipation, shovel to dig footing, a level, and impressive stakes from which even more impressive lines of string ran in reasonably straight configurations.

Footings that I had worked on in my lifetime wandering around the Midwest had always been two feet deep. Minimum. (When I had built our outdoor fireplace I had ignored this tradition, figuring that a little old thing like that didn't need any footing at all. The result was that the frost heaved the blamed thing up and toppled the concrete blocks into the middle by the third year. But that's another story.) But two feet seemed about half too much work, stones, and mortar, so I dug out only a foot of dirt, filled the ditch with rock, and worked cement into it, bringing it up to ground level. With my cement still wet, I laid into it the first run of stones. I intended to keep right on going, but found that I couldn't. As I laid on the third run of rocks, they started sliding off onto my toes. So every evening I put on another layer of rock and let the mortar dry. Next day, on this solid base, I slopped wet mortar, and stacked on another row of stones.

The wall grew ever so slowly, but my admiration for the builders of the Great Wall of China grew at great pace. I kept the width of the wall generally about eight inches, though it varied with whatever rock I happened to use next. I laid the rocks fairly even on one side, and let them stick out on the other as they pleased. I made five more trips to town for sand and cement.

It seemed like such a muddling job—it *was* a muddling job, yet miraculously, the finished part looked positively beautiful. Beauty being in the eye of the beholder. I even got a few compliments: "You mean *you* did that? I don't believe it."

I made one mistake that may become critical in the years to come. When you lay stones, the idea is to place the middle of a rock over the crack between the two right below it. This keeps a seam of cement from forming a single continuous line from top to bottom. My wall may someday crack right along one of these seams that I should not have allowed to form.

At the rate I am going, I will not have my wall finished for years, but it is very pleasant to look at the finished part. A poem I built in stone—a crude one, like all my peoms, but singularly my own. And when the cats sit on top of it, I feel I have added something to the world. Where did they sit before?

Of all the stupid things I have done in my lifetime, my fence-building has to rank very close to the top of the list. Some years ago I got into a fencing project in a swamp in Minnesota. How that came about is too involved and unbelievable to recount here. Parts of this swamp were utterly unfarmable, but parts were, at least most of the year, solid enough for a cow pasture. So I found myself making little fields in the swamp, around which fences were needed to keep cattle from blundering into the marsh and sinking up to their bellies. I wanted my fields to be rather precise geometric squares and rectangles, a tradition I grew up with in Ohio.

By the time I got to the last corner of the first rectangle, I found that the two lines of fence converged at a point off the solid ground, a bit into the more swampy area. However, the ground was still frozen there, and I was thinking about something else — probably quitting time. I punched a hole in that frozen earth, inserted the post, stretched the barbed wire, and nailed it on. Five days later, when the ground thawed into primordial ooze, the corner post simply fell over. You can't get any dumber than that.

Well, yes, you can too. Once I used some posts made out of dead elm logs, which rotted off in exactly one season.

Another time I was stretching a length of fence across a shallow valley. The fence line dipped down a slight slope and then back up again to the next corner post, so that the space between was shorter through the air than by land. When I stretched the woven wire fence, it raised off the ground nearly four feet at the bottom of the slope. With great effort, I pulled the fence down to the steel posts I had previously driven into the ground, and wired it fast. I was proud of that fence. It was stretched so tight you could almost strum a tune on it. Next spring, after the thaw, the upward tension of the fence pulled the steel posts all out of the ground at the bottom of the slope. Pigs scooted under it and scattered to the four corners.

When we lived in the log cabin, I hankered for a rail fence to fit the decor. I didn't have anything to fence in, so I wasn't worried about doing something practical — a talent I knew I didn't possess anyway. So I more or less propped up a rail fence. Getting the old rails was easy because there was a whole fence of them deteriorating away in the woods. I remembered reading that a rail fence had to be set up on rocks at each zig (or zag) where two sections of the fence join together. You do not set the bottom rail on one rock but on two. The reason for this is that moisture would work through one rock and rot the bottom rail, the old-timers maintained. The second rock acts as a vapor barrier. So I placed one flat rock atop another at each zig and zag of the fence, and laid on the first string of rails, then the second, the third, up to six high. Beautiful. Sometimes the rails would fall off because I had no posts sunk into the ground to anchor them, but finally I had the whole thing balanced together. A friend stopped by to admire it. Before I could stop him, he hunkered his backside up on the top rail, took the load off his feet, and a whole section of fence crumpled (with him) to the ground.

This required thought. I remembered dimly that some rail fences were strengthened with short posts wedged and braced solidly into the ground between the overlaps where two sections of rails joined. A little experimenting proved that two such rails slanted from the ground up between the overlaps and crossed on top did bind in the rails so that no single one could be knocked off.

A few days later, a huge dog came bounding through the woods, evidently on a hot trail of a rabbit. His nose to the ground, he followed the scent under the bottom rail of the fence. The opening, fine for rabbits, did not quite accommodate the dog. He pushed through anyway, and three complete sections of fence, all bound together, came crashing down.

My downfall usually results from Looking for an Easier Way. I once decided to harness the water of a creek for my own purposes without checking my plan against a background that included the creek at floodtime. I decided to construct an automatic irrigator. I had cleared a garden patch in the woods next to a very small creek through which a bare trickle of water flowed. (Let me digress to say also that you should never clear a patch in the woods for a garden. My patch was large enough, but when the leaves came out on the surrounding trees, the garden was completely shaded in except for about two hours a day. All my plants grew rapidly, straight up and spindly, trying to reach sunlight. They produced very little, and the wind blew many of them over. Do not try to garden in the woods.) I figured all I had to do was dam up the creek and dig a ditch diverting the water over into the garden nearby. Excellent. I built a dam, blocking the trickle. The water rose slowly. Some leaked away. By dark, it had risen to within six inches of my ditch. I went to bed visualizing the water softly oozing into my drought-suffering garden by morning.

Along about midnight, we were awakened by a steady pouring rain. It sounded beautiful. The drought was broken. I lay there, blissfully loving rain, until my mind slowly began to grasp the significance of cloudburst, dam, and diversion ditch.

I jumped out of bed. My wife said it had been raining steadily for an hour, and she could not figure out why I did not necessarily think that was good news. I suppose it took me another 15 minutes to get to my garden patch in the woods. The lantern showed that I built my dam well; it still held. Wading across the creek below it, I was appalled at what I saw. The tiny diversion ditch and the garden were a roaring rapids of muddy water. Quickly I raced back to the dam and tore away at it with numbed fingers. Not much tearing was needed. It quickly gave way and a wall of water descended on me and my lantern. Not that it mattered. The rain had all but drowned me already.

Not that the washed-out garden mattered either. Lack of sunlight had already sealed its doom.

The amount of water that runs off a watershed of even 50 acres in a year astounds prospective pond builders. When the soil conservationists tell them they need an over-flow pipe such-and-such a size and a spillway even bigger, the pond owner swears in disbelief. If he fails to listen to the experts he may lose half his dam in the first big storm. Having worked for the Soil Conservation Service in my wandering youth, I've seen it happen.

Another mistake of pond builders (nice to talk about

someone else's errors for a change), especially farmers, is to make use of a watershed above their pond that is being plowed and cultivated every year. I worked on such a pond. The farmer said, oh yes, he intended to plant the fields above the pond into pasture and hay. But he continued to grow corn there, and every rain washed literally tons of dirt into his pond and kept the water perennially muddy. But the man would not admit the error of his ways until it became unmistakably apparent that his pond was actually filling up with dirt, not water.

The pond my father built on our farm when I was a boy violated many of the rules of good pond building. The Soil Conservation Service agent offered to help and handed out a lot of free advice. My father didn't listen much. He never listened to anyone. I remember his comment was something like: "I know you boys know how to do this the right way, but the right way will end up costing me too much money, so I'll try it my way." In my own experience, this comment has always been prelude to disaster, but it seemed to work for Father. I guess he knew he had the most important pond-building commandments on his side. Only about 20 acres drained into the pond, all of it grass and woods. But the spillway was barely adequate for an overflowing mud puddle and he installed no overflow pipe at all, which sent the conservation agent into fits.

Father has never quite lost the dam, though it does leak through the bottom a little. His main trouble has been that the dam wasn't high enough to accommodate the muskrats. They would tunnel right through it, the water tumbling through behind them. After a few hairbreadth escapes in which we would get the hole plugged just before the whole dam let go, Father hauled more dirt to widen and raise the dam. The muskrats could then tunnel air holes to their dens without going all the way through the dam.

In the meantime, we tried desperately hard to rid our world of muskrats. When we nearly succeeded, the growth of cattails and other water weeds increased. Instead of perceiving ecological truth—that the 'rats ate the weeds —we waged chemical warfare on the plants. In doing so, we made the error that is probably the single, most important cause of pollution. We followed ancient principle which says: If a certain amount of something will accomplish a purpose, twice that amount will accomplish it better. It sure did. We cleaned out the weeds, the cattails, and almost all the fish.

My brother applied that principle to his sweet corn. If the prescribed amount of herbicide would rid the corn of most weeds for a certain period of time, he reasoned that double that amount would kill all the weeds for even longer. His logic was unassailable. Weeds didn't grow in that plot for two years. Nor anything else. He called it his desert garden.

There are any number of ways that we applied our wonderful principle. If one stick of dynamite properly placed will blow out a stump, four sticks, even improperly placed, ought to blow it out even better. Quite right. Also three windows out of the chicken coop.

If one tractor couldn't move a heavy hayrack frozen in the mud, two could. Right again. But it took two trips. Only half of the stubborn rack came loose on the first pull.

If a little fertilizer makes pole beans climb vigorously, a lot of it should make the vines fairly leap up the poles. It worked. All vines, no beans.

Transplanting trees that are too large to transplant is *my* forte. In fact, the yearning for instant shade has led to my downfall as a landscaper. Time and again I have proved to my satisfaction that moving small trees or growing seedlings in place is easier and provides less chance for the tree to die. Also, the small tree invariably grows faster and catches up with the large transplant anyway. But I still try to move 15-foot trees.

I suffer through the same procedure every time. I start carefully, hoping to preserve a nice bunch of roots underneath the unlucky specimen. I dig and dig and dig. The tree remains firmly rooted down in China somewhere. After an hour, each spadeful of dirt merely knocks more soil away from exposed roots. I try to shove a burlap bag down under the excavation to preserve a ball of earth around the roots. It is like trying to thread a needle with a log chain. I tug on the tree trunk. Each heave lets more dirt fall out of the "ball."

In desperation, I get the tractor and wrap a cable around the trunk and begin to pull . . . gently. The cable slips and strips a foot of bark off the poor tree. This will never do. I unhook. Dig and curse a little longer. I give one last gut-wrenching heave, a taproot snaps loose somewhere in the bowels of the earth, and the tree comes flying out of the hole on top of me, its few remaining miserable roots completely bare. I rush the maimed thing to its new hole, sock it in, fill the hole with water and the best of topsoil. The tree stands there for three weeks. Four small, green leaves show halfway up its scarred trunk. The end.

I have a good neighbor who spends all his time and effort making things to save time and effort. He wanted to move a tree growing next to his house because it was threatening to push the roof gutter up in line with the chimney. Also, he needed some instant shade out in the yard. Why not move the tree and kill two birds with one stone?

He began to dig. There had to be an easier way. There was. He had engineered a boom affair attached to the hydraulic lift on his farm tractor that he used to lift heavy objects. He hooked it onto the tree, the boom rose, bent like a fishing pole lifting a ten-pound carp. The hydraulic pump sputtered, the tree held fast. Seizing his ax, my friend began to hack away at the resisting roots. All of a sudden, touché! The ax cleaved through the tap-root. Boom and tree flew heavenward, caught the roof gutter, and wrenched it free from the house into an imposing upside-down V for victory. Moral: Two dead birds are more worthless than a stone in the bush.

And while I am garbling a few proverbs, I might end this collection of travesties with another: He who laughs last never built a better mousetrap.

Chapter 16

Don't Look Now, But There's a Pig in Your Petunias

Books on gardening are replete with detailed advice on plants, but most of them assume that the gardener is not interested in the handmaiden art of husbandry. This is hardly ever true for the Two Acre Edenite. He wants to know which animals, if any, he can raise prudently on his amount of space. So I am going to try to reduce the experience of 30 years of living with animals of all kinds to a few hopefully helpful observations.

I am not going to tell you in detail how to raise all these animals, because each would make a book in itself, and there are plenty of those books already. I would caution you to read them with certain reservations. Many of them are written for commercial livestockmen, and the rules they give aren't always the same for the person who just wants a few for fun or food. And books have a tendency to make simple things sound complicated and complicated things simple.

I will just give you a very opinionated guide to livestock for the homestead of one acre or more. You won't agree with everything I say, I'm sure. Do it your own way, and then argue with me.

The first question you must answer in livestock raising is: Am I too softhearted? The purpose of livestock, generally, is for consumption, not for pets. Cats and dogs are pets. Whatever else you decide to raise, be it a chicken, rabbit, or calf, you, and especially your family, will become attached to it, adopt it, and be unable to slaughter it when the time comes. If you are so tenderhearted as not to be able to overcome this weakness, quit before you start and be content to watch the birds and squirrels. If you don't, you will end up with a circus menagerie in the backyard that will cost you money and the friendship of all your neighbors.

We have been through this ordeal in our family and have solved the problem this way. From the very beginning we tell the kids: "This chicken is for eating; this cat is a pet. This rabbit is yours till it dies of old age, but its offspring are for dinner." Stick to your resolution. You will find that your first butchering day is the hardest; your children will, after the first specter of death, accept it all in a proper spirit and will not, as some pseudo-psychologists try to say, become calloused by brutality. They will remain just as tender and sensitive to Life as ever, depending of course upon your own example. Farm boys of my generation are among the most sensitive and refined people I know, yet they were all brought up when butchering was a weekly affair.

I've already mentioned chickens as the perfect companion to good gardening and good eating, so I feel committed to tell you the easiest, cheapest way of raising them. The books say a chicken needs a minimum of two square feet of coop space. Just double that, since you are not out to make a fortune off the chicken business. The more space your hens have, the healthier they'll be, generally speaking. A dozen layers in a 10-by-20 building is about right. If you keep a foot of litter on the bare floor and add a little fresh bedding on the top every month, you will have no mess or odor, and you will have to clean out the coop only once a year.

We start out with 25 chicks, which we get in June when it's hot, so we have no need for any brooder equipment at all. Chicks need water and feed right away. Bread and milk are very good for them. We feed some commercial mash from the first day because modern formulas contain many nutrients chicks need. We usually keep them in a huge cardboard box for awhile on the enclosed porch, letting them run on the lawn within the confines of a roll of one-foot-high chicken fence during the day. When they outgrow the box, we shift them to a small coop. And when they outgrow that they go into the big coop, but separated from the old hens. When they grow large enough so the old hens won't chase them away from the feed trough, we take down the dividing fence. In the meantime, we have butchered all the old hens as they went into molt and quit laying eggs. Of the young brood, the roosters and all but about ten of the best hens are butchered as broilers and fryers starting in November. Usually, a few of the older hens remain healthy layers, so we go into the winter with about a dozen laying hens.

Don't keep hens much more than two years. Keep your stock young and vigorous. Don't try to nurse a sick hen back to health. The best medicine for a sick hen is the ax. Bury her in the garden where she will make good fertilizer. You can build a run for the chickens to wander in outside. But they will merely turn it into an ugly patch of bare ground. We let ours out occasionally on sunny days about two hours before sundown. They won't roam far enough to make all our neighbors angry and will return to roost as soon as it gets dark.

Feed them all your garbage, all the garden stuff you can't get used, plus a little grain and mash. In winter we get scrap lettuce leaves from the grocery for them. I get permission from farmers to glean their cornfields after harvest for stray ears that the corn picker missed. (Good excuse to hike the fields looking for Indian relics.) I always feed the hens some commercial mash even if I don't have to, because it contains so many elements I'm not sure the hens get otherwise.

If you have a small farm, you can let chickens run (but they will get in the garden and take one peck out of every ripe tomato), and they will balance their own diets splendidly. Keep oystershells before the hens at all times, and grit too, if you have to keep them penned up most of the time, as I do. Keep fresh water before them constantly. Hay made from the clover in your lawn is a good winter source of protein, often overlooked, for chickens and rabbits.

It is much easier to overfeed than underfeed, and that is how some people lose money on their hens. Hens should clean up all feed given in the morning by the evening, if not sooner. You'll just kind of learn.

Buckets and boxes make good nests. The nest should be dark inside. Hens like it better that way, and they don't get a chance to stare at the eggs so clearly that they get the idea of eating one. If they do eat eggs, it is usually a sign of calcium deficiency (they need oystershells), but sometimes it is just a sign of pure orneriness.

Chickens are prone to a vast number of diseases, but ours have always been healthy following these simple methods. If trouble should develop, I'd get rid of the whole bunch, disinfect the coop, and, after a couple of months, start all over. There is no use messing around with sick chickens.

Raising your own chickens is not supposed to save you money, but we certainly do. The value of the chickens we eat pays for the feed we have to buy up until that time. And then some. The eggs we sell pay for the feed from then on. And then some. Our eggs (and the manure) we get for free.

A cow has to be milked every morning and every evening, come hell or high water. If, after a little thought, that is not enough to discourage you completely you are a real, genuine believer in Two Acre Edens.

A cow has several stomachs, and as the food she eats travels through them, it seems to grow in bulk rather than being assimilated into her body, if one measures the amount of manure she produces. If you have one cow, you almost need to have two, so that when one goes dry, the other keeps you supplied with milk. If you do not pasteurize the milk, you must be sure your cow is free of brucellosis and tuberculosis. If you do not have a bull around (and you shouldn't), you will need to have the artificial inseminator stop by once or twice a year. Gestation, freshening, drying up, and all that is just too much for me to go into here. If you do not know cows, it won't make much practical sense, and if you do know cows, you'll buy your milk from the milkman and keep your mouth shut.

But I must say something nice about cows, because actually, they are my favorite animals. I lived with them literally for more years than I care to remember and I'm still living with them. If you have five or more acres, like to be home every day, and are really hooked on raising your own food, a couple of cows can keep you in meat, milk, butter, and cottage cheese (maybe other cheeses) and save you money if you have a large family. I would suggest, if you are crazy enough to still want a cow, that you buy a Jersey or Guernsey—smaller breeds that give less but richer milk.

If you milk your cows by hand, more power to you. If you have a teenage son, tell him there is positively no better way to develop good wrists for hitting baseballs and throwing footballs. However, if he isn't interested in playing in the World Series, you can find a small, portable milking machine reasonably priced. In fact, you may be able to get a used machine for nearly nothing from a dealer, since this type of unit is obsolete in commercial dairying.

With the way food prices are now, you can save money with a cow even if you have to buy all the feed. If your paradise is five acres, have a pasture for your cows. That alone will save you a healthy part of your feed bill through the summer. Cows like grass and legumes and chopped-up green corn and chopped-up dry corn fodder, and chopped-up pumpkins, and certain kinds of root crops like mangels and sugar beets. In New Zealand, dairymen "graze" cows on mangels when the grass gives out, which is a very slick idea you cannot appreciate unless you have handled 5 million hay bales, as I have.

If you get into the cow business and don't know what you are doing, ask the farmer down the road. What he tells you may or may not be correct, but it is better than total ignorance. Eventually, your cow will train you very well indeed.

A more practical idea, if you have the room, is to buy a young steer (that's a castrated bull calf), preferably of a beef variety, and feed it for a while. If you buy one around 300 to 400 pounds in the spring, feed and graze it till fall, it ought to weight upward of 800 pounds. You can go ahead and finish it out with heavy grain feeding to a choice 1,200 pounds, but that may start costing you money. Even at lighter weights, the meat will generally taste as good as or better than what you can buy. If you don't know how to butcher the animal, you can usually find someone in the area who does. If you promise him some choice T-bone steaks and dangle a fifth of good bourbon, he will generally deign to help you do the job. Try to keep the bourbon unopened until the butchering is almost completed.

Even counting in the bourbon, you ought to come out ahead on this little project unless you were feeding your steer caviar.

If you decide to raise bovines, make sure your fences are strong enough to stop tanks and tight enough to outwit a Houdini. I once chased ten steers (unfortunately my own) through a small town. Not only was the experience harrowing, but I narrowly missed several lawsuits that would have cost me more than all the steers combined were worth.

A riding horse has one advantage. It does not make as much noise as a motorcycle. If you have the land and a teenage daughter, the horse question will take care of itself. You have my sympathy. And a pony is even worse than a horse. Do not even think of putting more than one horse on less than two acres, unless you plan to buy *all* the horse's feed. A horse will tramp a half-acre lot into a mud wallow, chew all the wood in its stall to sawdust, break down the fence and run over your neighbor's garden. If you get sued, you deserve it.

If you can keep him contained inside a good fence, a pig is a practical livestock venture for a small homestead. But your zoning regulations may prohibit hogs. A pig is a smart and very clean animal by nature, but some hog feeders crowd too many of his brothers inadequately in small pens, and the resulting aroma has ruined his reputation in outer suburbia. But many pigs are raised under conditions that are nearly as clean as those under which many human babies are raised.

Go to a good hog farmer and buy your pig after it has been weaned. Take it home and feed it what the farmer told you to feed it. If he did not mention table scraps and good alfalfa hay, he just forgot to. In fact your pig will eat just about anything, but he likes corn best of all. If you let him run in a lot, he will root up parts of it into an unsightly wallow. If that bothers you, you can keep him penned up or put a ring in his nose.

Pigs, with encouragement, become friendly pets, and if they do, they like to be where you are. At that stage, they can find a way to get through or under almost any fence made by man. Then they will run into the yard outside your door, and squeal in a most pitiable and lovable way. A pet pig is an excellent gift for your enemies.

It's best to keep the pig in a barn, in a roomy, clean pen. If they have enough space, hogs will deposit their manure in one end of the pen and keep their living quarters relatively clean. That is how smart they are. Naturally housebroken. My sister fattens a hog every year in her backyard in a ten-by-ten pen made of slatted two by sixes for the floor and snow fence walls. She hoses the pen down every day — the manure falls through the slatted floor that is raised two feet off the ground.

When your pig approaches 180 pounds, butcher it. You can tell the weight by standing on scales and weighing yourself, then stand on it again holding the pig, and subtract. Good luck.

Seriously, you can butcher a pig anytime: when it's small, if you want to barbecue a whole "suckling" pig, on up to six months, when it will weigh about 200 pounds, or at nine months when it weighs up to 300 pounds.

An excellent idea is to get together with any like-minded pig-raising neighbors and have an old-fashioned butchering day. A good time will be had by all, but I have found that as an adult doing the work, butchering day is not quite as jolly as I remembered it as a child. All I did then was tend the fire under the iron lard tubs, get sick eating too many "cracklings," and sneak drinks of Grandpaw's applejack.

As long as you are going to all the trouble of butchering, you probably would like to know how to smoke ham and bacon correctly. I am going to tell you whether you want to know or not, because I am afraid this gentle art is being lost. Some future generation with a better sense of values than ours may want to know.

Here's how to smoke a ham the "perfect" way, not taken from some other book, but from the actual process of an old Kentucky farmer who has been doing it for 70 years, and whom I have watched do it for 10 years, and whose ham has made my mouth water in unspeakable delight.

First you get the hams. The perfect ones come from hogs that have been fattened slowly, if at all, on a diet of ear corn, acorns, and whatever else the animal could forage from woodland and ridges. This kind of hog hardly exists anymore. Hogs today are all fed on diets of commercial feeds that fatten them to marketable size in five months. The difference between a ham from this hog and a ham from a rangy ridge runner is undetectable by mere mortals. Only those privileged few, fortunate enough to have received the finest cultural advantages of the Appalachian Mountains (hillbillies) understand these niceties of civilization. Such a ham from a razorback hog has a certain timbre, texture, and flavor unequaled by any modern ham.

But anyhow, get what hams you can get. Each ham should weigh about 20 pounds, which means it came from a hog that weighed, alive, about 200 pounds. If you are buying the hams, rather than butchering your own, buy them directly from the butcher before he has done anything except cool them. Hams should be cured and smoked in the fall before cold weather arrives—"allus before Christmas" in Kentucky. The entire process takes about six weeks, depending on the weather.

Lay your hams on a table, the hide side down. (We skin our hogs, so there is no hide side.) Mix about 5½ cups of salt, 1 pound, 10 ounces of brown sugar, and 2 ounces of black pepper together for two hams and two sides of bacon and vigorously rub this curing mixture into the meat. Some people shoot a liquid salt solution into the ham around the hambone with a hypodermic needle, but this is unnecessary if you do everything else right.

Rub the curing mixture into each ham and bacon slab for about ten minutes. Then lay them all together, but not touching, and spread about a ⅜-inch-thick layer of the mixture over all the hams (hide side still down). Then tilt the table just a wee bit, so that the melting brine will be able to drain off the meat. Let the hams sit for 4 to 5 weeks and the bacon about 10 to 12 days. If the weather is unusually warm for late fall, the shorter time is enough; if unusually cold, the longer time is necessary.

Then scrub off the curing mixture with warm water and a brush. Carefully puncture a very small hole through the hock, run a heavy string (untainted by any kind of dye or preservative) through the hole, and hang the meat in a smokehouse.

You don't have a smokehouse? Any structure that measures about eight feet by six feet and has a ceiling eight feet or nine feet from the floor will do. You can build a temporary enclosure. (I've used a long, narrow fireplace with a piece of tin over it to hold in the smoke—the hams at one end, the fire at the other. Now I use a steel 55-gallon drum that draws smoke from a smoldering hickory fire ten feet away.) The hams should hang at least five feet from the fire. The wood should be green apple or hickory and should smolder, not burn brightly. The hams must not get hot, or they may spoil later on.

Remember that the smoking process was used originally to preserve the meat. The smoke and heat seal the ham, and that keeps it from spoiling. The fact that smoking also results in a good-tasting ham was incidental to the original purpose. Warm, cloudy weather is best for smoking. Smoke the ham for six days, eight hours a day, the bacon three to four days. By that time, your meat will have taken on a golden glow. Then wrap each piece in a heavy paper sack, a grade or two heavier than an ordinary grocery sack, and twist the top tightly shut so no bugs can get in. If possible hang the hams under a roof that absorbs heat from the sun. The heat continues to drive the salt into the ham. The ham will not freeze, mice or other varmints will not be able to get to it if it is hung right, and theoretically, it is preserved for years. Ideally the ham should hang there and season for a year, but if you get hungry you can eat it sooner. We now hang ours in the cellar, and they do fine.

The ham tastes best if cooked in this manner: Put it in a pot with water about halfway up the ham. Let it come up to a simmer, pour the water off, and bake at 300 degrees F. for about 20 minutes to the pound. If the ham weighs 20 pounds that's about 6½ hours. Serve cold the next day. You will have brought paradise one step closer to reality.

I will not say much about goats, since I never personally raised any. Most books on subsistence farming maintain that goats are more practical than cows. This is especially true where people are tubercular or allergic to cow's milk and *must* drink goat's milk. Goat's milk is more digestible than cow's.

If you have several acres of grass going to waste, and if beef cattle or hogs aren't your bag, give sheep a try. Actually, in this situation, sheep are more practical in many ways. First of all, you don't have to milk them. Second, they make much better lawn mowers than cows. Sheep keep weeds down better, and can utilize such cheap feed better than beef animals. You can usually graze about four to five sheep to the acre. But as a noncommercial sheepman, you'd be smart to figure three head per acre. Better to have too much grass than not enough. Besides your ewes may have twins or triplets.

On the farm, we used to figure that sheep paid off more profit *for the time we put in them,* than any other livestock on the farm. I think that is still true. If you like lamb chops, and have a couple of acres going to waste, a ram and two ewes should be your next buy. You need a good fence, but it need not be as sturdy as for cattle or hogs.

Lambs are fun to watch, too. A group of them will play tag just about like children. But sheep seem to be stupid. I've known ewes that stuck their heads through a fence and did. not have enough sense to back out. They just kept trying to push ahead until they starved to death. When I was a kid, we used to be glad when a sheep died. We were allowed to pick the wool from any carcass we found in the pastures and sell it. Heck of a way to make a living.

One of the few disadvantages with sheep, especially in more settled areas, is that dogs like to chase them—at least some dogs do. In the "old days"—and actually the custom is still strong in sheep country—any dog caught chasing sheep was summarily shot, no questions asked. I lost my dog that way. Only he wasn't chasing sheep. He was chasing a neighbor's purebred hound. But the neighbor said the dog was in the sheep, and the tradition was so sacred that it protected the lie. A boy who has lost his dog remembers . . . forever.

Anyway, I think in suburbia, all loose running dogs should be summarily shot, even if they are only chasing rainbows. If one gets in your sheep, sting him with a shotgun loaded with salt—or buckshot from a sufficient distance so as not to hurt him much. The law is on your side, as they say. You can still (but I wonder for how much longer?) protect your own property.

Remember that a sheep produces wool, too—maybe $12 or more a clip. Lamb chops sometimes get as high as $3.50 a pound in the supermarket. And to me a sack of sheep manure is worth about as much as a sack of any fertilizer. Imagine a lawn mower that pays *you*.

I do not advise you to try to shear a sheep unless you know how. There are professional sheep shearers in every rural community. They are very hard to find if you have only a few sheep. They make more money clipping their way through *big* flocks. Look very wise and pay whatever they charge you. If the bill is more than a quarter of the wool's value, you are probably getting cheated a little, but it is not worth quibbling about. Maybe you can find an FFA youngster in the neighborhood who knows how to shear sheep. Or have him teach you. I can't think of a better way to tune up for a yoga lesson.

Rabbits are a natural for the small homestead. Breeds like the New Zealand make excellent meat. Build your hutches and make your nest boxes *exactly* according to whatever instructions you follow. There is a reason for everything. A mother rabbit is an extremely nervous creature sometimes, and if everything isn't just so, she will kill her offspring or refuse to care for them.

Like chickens, there are many unusual kinds of rabbits in this country—58 recognized breeds. Rabbit pelts are worth a little money (not much). Some rabbit fanciers are interested only in trying to develop a better fur. But buyers seem to prefer white to other colors. You can make a very interesting hobby out of rabbit genetics. For instance, there is a recessive gene that produces a shorter, thicker fur than usual. It's called the "rex" factor, and pelts of this kind, after being quite undesirable for years, are now drawing interest from buyers again.

One hardly thinks of earthworms as a type of livestock, but on worm ranches, that is exactly what they are. I've always been inclined to group worms and chinchillas and ginseng and such ilk in the category of "Yes-it-will-make-you-some-money-if-you-find-suckers-to-buy-your-breeding-stock." But just the other day, I received a letter from a woman who went into the worm business, concentrating on the bait market, and she is doing right well. Organic gardeners buy earthworms too, to improve their gardens.

Some rabbit growers have found that worms are a good companion crop for them. They place worm beds right under the rabbit hutches. Droppings from the rabbits fall into the beds, and the worms grow vigorously on them. The worm droppings (called "castings" in polite society), make a wonderfully fertile potting soil, which some greenhouse owners will buy.

If you are fortunate enough to have a pond or stream on your property, fresh fish can be a staple in your diet — and provide hours of fun. A cold, swift-running stream can be adapted for trout (or vice versa) and the warmer water of a pond makes a good home for bass. When or if you stock a pond with bass, stock it with bass, period. Largemouth bass. No chubs. No bluegills. Just bass. Some wildlife "experts" still insist on a mixture of bass and blue-gills. Don't listen to them. The bluegills overpopulate too fast. If you can get big bass — like a pound or more in size — so much the better. Largemouth bass are cannibalistic. They will eat minnows of their own species. This keeps your fish population from exploding. As the young bass reach six inches in length, start fishing the heck out of them. In an overcrowded pond, you get a whole bunch of small fish; no big ones. The more you fish, the better. Now most experts generally concede that it is nearly impossible to overfish a pond unless you use a net. Stock channel catfish with bass. The catfish will not reproduce. But it's better to add more fish occasionally than to have a crowded pond.

Another kind of "livestock" you should raise around your pond is bullfrogs. If you get a pair of them to settle down, the population will slowly rise until you can harvest a meal or two or more every year. Frog hunting is considered by many to be as much fun as fishing.

Snapping turtles are so good to eat that I wish I could tell you to do the same with them as with bullfrogs. Unfortunately, snapping turtles grow very slowly. You almost have to take them as they come in the wild. I fear that there are too many people like myself who know how good turtle meat is (not turtle soup—that's for tourists) and are catching them faster than they can reproduce. Anyway, the turtles will eat small frogs and crayfish (crayfish tails are very good too—just miniature lobster tails) and keep down the population of these critters. If you know a place where you can get real live snapping turtles, get some for your pond. You'll get other kinds of turtles by natural migration, and perhaps even a snapper, too.

Your pond will also attract ducks, geese, and musk-rats. All are good to eat, by the way. The muskrats are worth trapping for two reasons: They can ruin your pond dam and their pelts are salable. You might even trap a mink who will come looking for a muskrat. But keep a few "rats in residence," as I've said, to help control water weeds in the pond.

Just a few months ago I visited a gardener who had constructed his own small creek through his garden on his three-quarter-acre lot. Water flows down rapids he made out of cement studded with rocks, through a series of pools (one with an island in it), and finally into a last, quite deep pool. There the water is drawn out through a bottom drain and pumped (the pump is underground and out of sight and makes no noise) back up to the beginning of the "creek" where it gurgles over some rocks like a waterfall and flows on to the other end again. Goldfish swim in the deeper pools. (I don't know why he has this hang-up with goldfish. He should keep bass or catfish in there, or something decent to eat.) The creek is a neat idea if you don't have a real one. You can simply shut it off in the winter. And it is always clean. It sounds just like a real brook splashing by. And that is a very good sound.

Summing up: On two acres or less stick with chick-ens and rabbits. On three acres you can add a summer-fattened hog, if you build a good pen. On four acres add two ewes and a ram, or a couple of goats if you have a good fence. On five or more acres and with lots of dedica-tion, try a milk cow. If you lack dedication, feed out a steer. Riding horses and large dogs are luxuries that belong only on larger homesteads.

Chapter 17

Schemes (Some Slightly Harebrained) to Make Money on the Side

There is no magazine or newspaper, however devoid of the true interests of the countryman, that isn't saved by the classified ads. Only here does the individuality and native originality of the American people show itself in its true light. Here is America unexpurgated; here are pathos, tragedy, dreams of grandeur; here are lovers' trysts, meetings of the lonely, answered prayers. Here is something for everyone.

Want a date? A free (almost) ride to California? A dependable wife who is a good cook? Want to know how to destroy moles? Where to buy a windmill or cider press? How to gross $50 a day making concrete fence posts? Like goat's-milk ice cream? Organic yogurt? Jerusalem artichokes? Canadian firewood? Honey? Want to make a small fortune raising red wigglers? Or ginseng? How about a biblical secret that will make you a notable success for life? Any yen to be a millionaire? A homesteader in Yucatán? A gem hunter?

Buy the "little" magazines and newspapers you run across and read the classified ads. There's somebody, somewhere, making a little money on anything you can possibly imagine. And a few things that you can't imagine.

But obey the rules of the game. The ads are to be read, savored, dreamed about, and only rarely acted upon. It takes faith to enjoy the classified ads—a faith without credulity.

This owner and/or dreamer of Two Acre Eden is hooked on classified ads. I won't admit it, but somewhere deep in my psyche there is a conviction that I really could make a living right off my little homestead. Or at least make enough money to pay the taxes—any more would be quite an accomplishment. Someplace buried in someone's classified ad is the germ of an idea that could be developed into my Thing. Someday I will find it.

If you are searching too, you may find this chapter a good companion piece to read. Having been on the less affluent side of the tracks all my life (I keep crossing over only to find that there are only more tracks ahead, which I am still on the wrong side of), I love the make-it-pay psychology. Therefore I've collected some schemes that might add a little money to your Two Acre Eden treasury. Most of these ideas have been tried by me or someone I know with varying degrees of success.

Whenever you begin to think of profits from a Two Acre Eden, the roadside stand comes onto the mental horizon. Roadside-stand operations are the darlings of writers who want to show you how to make a living from a small acreage. Especially writers who haven't tried to run one. Theoretically at least their arguments make some sense, especially today. Why?

(1) Because people are running scared from food additives and chemicals—they're looking for better-quality fresh food. (2) Because people are more mobile today and like to have an excuse to take a ride in the country. Roadside-stand shopping has become a very popular excuse. (3) Because the small farmer-gardener must be able to sell retail to make an appreciable profit.

For these reasons, and others, many roadside operations are extremely successful. But be aware that we are talking about a Business now — an operation requiring hired labor, considerable overhead, good location, long, long hours, and a love for people that must be nearly divine. A good roadside-stand business is a great idea, if you have these capacities, together with a detailed knowledge of retail marketing and horticulture. Believe me, it's no place for an amateur. Moreover, the peace and plenty of your Two Acre Eden will be shattered irreparably.

On the other hand, if you like to set a card table up along the road on weekends, or when you just happen to have something to sell, you can have some fun and even make a little money. In this light, most of the suggestions that follow can be marketed along the road. I think the idea is especially good if you have sons and daughters old enough to wait on customers. They will learn a lot about people, and if they know they are earning a little money of their *own*, they will learn something about life, too. And maybe help you help them get through college.

Rather than having a roadside stand on Two Acre Eden, I believe that it is generally more practical to sell extra produce to a few regular customers. If, for example, you sell eggs to five or ten families who buy yours because they appreciate quality, these same people are prime prospects for your other products. It is not too hard to work up a clientele of ten such discerning families, each of whom would buy at least $100 worth of stuff from you every year if you had it. These kinds of people usually love to pick their own fruits and vegetables if invited to do so. You can train them to do the job right and they will keep your back from getting sore. If you allow families to go into your henhouse and gather their own eggs, they will be absolutely delighted. But you may have to teach their children how to behave around plants and animals.

If, on the other hand, you don't want to be bothered by customers dropping in all the time, you can work up a delivery route to these selected few and it won't take too much of your time.

People who appreciate good food will pay for quality. Keep your prices right up there with the chain stores, or a little higher. But be generous. When they buy a dozen ears of corn, make sure the sack contains 14. If they buy some high-priced melons, give them some string beans. The beans will probably go to waste anyway.

Your biggest problem will be keeping down the number of customers to equal the amount of work you want to do. When the word gets out, you'll have more customers than you can handle.

With that as background, let's work our way through the year and see what we can make in petty cash every month. But keep a grain or two of salt handy.

January: If the snow's not deep, now is the time to saw and split fireplace wood to sell to the lovers of the open hearth. Demand is greatest during the Thanksgiving-Christmas-New Year holidays, but you have to cut it now so it will season well by next fall. Besides, there's nothing much else to do on Two Acre Eden during the cold winds of January.

Another good way to forget the weather is to cheer yourself up with some profit-making plans you want — you want *surely* — to try sometime, someplace.

Here is a dilly I thought up all by myself. I share it with you only out of a deep feeling for the well-being of my fellowman.

Why not corner the market on papaws? Since the demand is not exactly heavy right now that should be no trouble. But seriously, when is the last time you ate a good, ripe, mouth-watering papaw?

Papaws grow wild from the South on up through the Midwest as far north as Michigan, where some people call them Michigan bananas. You can find them wild in New York, New Jersey, and Pennsylvania too. West Virginia has a town called Paw Paw.

Papaws aren't everyone's ice cream and cake. Gourmets maintain that the fruit is downright scrumptious if allowed to fall from the tree in the autumn and lie in the leaves for a week. By this time the color has changed from yellow to brown. Skin and eat it.

But real natives of papaw country make a ritual

out of eating the fruit. First they knead the papaw, skin intact, to soften the pulp—the way some people do with oranges. Then they cut off or bite off one end of the papaw and suck out the inside.

Man, it's soul food. Papaws are part of our culture, complete with old traditional recipes and folklore that run all the way back to the Indians. So what if they don't taste as good as real bananas?

If you can't sell papaws as gourmet food, you ought to be able to sell them as ornamental plants. The papaw is actually a tropical plant, but a hardy one. Its huge leaves remind you of the jungle. The flowers are green in spring, turning to a velvety purple. The fruit is yellow. What gardener could resist it?

Several of the mail-order nurseries sell papaw trees. But no mad advertising genius has pushed them in years. Here's your chance. Actually—seriously—a few small nurserymen have selected and propagated choice strains of wild papaw. They tell me they can sell all they can produce—at ten dollars a tree currently.

By the way, papaws don't fruit every year. Look at it optimistically. Not fruiting every year keeps your poorman's bananas a highly desirable gourmet rarity.

Or in the off years, sell persimmons. Grafted trees of selected wild strains are selling well too.

February: If you have survived the woodcutting venture and are still game for offbeat ideas, now is the time to try making and selling maple syrup. The advantage of this is that you will probably get enough to enjoy once on your own table anyway. Sugaring is a very sophisticated commercial enterprise nowadays, but don't let that deter you. Real maple syrup is expensive.

First you need some trees, of course. Maple trees are best, especially sugar maple, but other varieties produce sap with an appreciable sugar content.

Drill a hole—a half-inch in diameter—in the tree to a depth of about two inches. Then, stick a spile or spout in the hole. I use a sumac stem, forming a hollow tube. (Is there any other kind of tube?) Or you can split the stem and use half of it for a spile. The sap will run out the end and drip into your bucket. I have been setting my buckets on the ground under the spile, but dogs may upset them, or do something worse. Hang your buckets out of harm's way. Frosty nights and warm, thawing days make the sap run well and you should get a couple of gallons a day from each tree.

Boiling the sap down is the only hard part of the job, really. If you try to boil down much more than a few gallons on the stove, the steam will begin to drip from walls and ceilings. People have been known to lose wallpaper that way.

Do the job outside, using a broad, shallow pan. If you burn wood, it is very romantic—but it takes a lot of wood. Unless you have an ample supply, it is far better to rig up an oil or kerosene burner. Boil until only syrup is left, a little on the thin side for pancakes. If you boil longer the thickened syrup will, upon drying, be sugar. If you boil longer than that, as we did a couple of times, you have nothing but a scorched pan. You can sell your syrup for the same price the genuine stuff is going for in the grocery store, and that's quite a bit. Having gone through this process, you will understand why. And having tasted real maple syrup, you will also understand that it's worth it.

March: If you have a meadow (I've been asking for a meadow for Christmas ever since I left the farm), you should plant it to snowdrops—dotted all over the field— in the fall. Then in blustery, cold, barren March, you will have a whole carpet of dainty white flowers.

People passing by will be delighted. They will stop and ask if they can have some.

You say, sure they can, but they will have to wait until you dig them some—at a dollar a clump. When you dig them, though, be very careful to take plants only where the clumps are already too crowded, leaving enough so that what is left can continue to increase and spread. This is a fairly original harebrained idea. I can't see why it wouldn't work.

Schemes to Make Money on the Side

By the end of March the daffodils are growing, but daffodils are so easy to raise, there isn't much money in it for people like you and me. I know a chap though, who plans ahead for those Easters that come early in the spring, before daffodils bloom naturally. On such years, he pots a bunch of them and puts them in his warm cellar in February. The plants grow in the dark, all yellow without sunlight. Then about ten days before Easter he puts them out in a protected, sunlit spot — all along the south side of his garage. The leaves green up and the buds open right in time for Easter — $1.50 a pot. I know another commercial grower who forces daffodils this way in a cave. It's a trick you can use when you don't have a greenhouse.

April: This is a bad month for a sideline income from the soil. You will be busy with spring work, but there is nothing growing in the garden that is edible except rhubarb. I think it is a good month to be selling birdhouses made out of all those crazy gourds still hanging on the trellises in the garden.

You don't grow gourds? You should. There are many varieties, but only certain types make good birdhouses, mostly the species of the *Lagenaria* genus whose various types go by names like Dipper, Siphon, Powder Horn, Chinese Water Jug, Dolphin. These gourds have an enduring hard shell. The smaller gourds usually rot after a month or so, but *Lagenaria*, dried properly, will last any number of years. You can paint, wax, or shellac them and make all kinds of wall or coffee-table decorations out of them. Some people get atrocious results. Every year at least one of the garden magazines carries an article on gourds or on someone who makes a few pennies selling gourd birdhouses.

May: An awfully busy month, especially since one should spend as much time as possible roaming through the woods, along creeks, over the hills, just enjoying life. May is asparagus month, and asparagus is one of the most practical things you can grow — and sell. Asparagus requires little labor to raise and once established and cared for will last about as long as you will. Asparagus is especially important to the selling gardener because there isn't anything else going for him in May that people want to eat, except — as in April — rhubarb. Asparagus is no good unless it is absolutely fresh, another advantage for the roadside retailer. Lots of people don't like the vegetable because they've never eaten any right out of the garden.

June: It is tragic, a condemnation of all humanity, that people have to work in June. You would think that with all our knowledge and scientific prowess, man would have been able to invent some method whereby work in June was unnecessary. June should be spent floating on a slight breeze just above a clover field. It should be spent making love and writing poems and dabbling at random in field and garden. But it never works that way. June in the country is all bustle.

June is for eating strawberries. Anyone industrious enough to raise and harvest a crop won't have any trouble selling them. But it's hard work. You have to plant strawberries every year — or should — and weed, mulch, and pray over them. Pruning the runners back the first year to only five or six per plant and pinching blossoms off the first year is hard work and time-consuming, but you will get berries much larger the second or main crop year, and thus reduce the time it takes to pick a quart. Picking strawberries for someone other than yourself isn't much fun, no matter how much they pay for them. But you can't raise anything that will sell better. Here's where I use my pick-them-yourself scheme.

July: Now come raspberries. I rank raspberries with asparagus as a practical profitmaker, because raspberries require less work than strawberries. For one thing, you don't have to bend over as far to pick them, so your back will hold up a little longer. For another, a raspberry patch ought to last eight years at least. If you are going to raise raspberries, I advise you solemnly to have some means of getting water to them other than from the sky. Along about the time they are beginning to ripen, the weather often turns dry and can cut yields in half. Heavy mulch can sometimes substitute for irrigation.

Some people like black raspberries, some like red.

And to me, the yellow and purple ones taste best of all. People aren't used to the latter, except in some areas, and won't buy them. If you get serious about raspberries, sell blacks and reds in July, then have another patch of ever-bearing red raspberries that you prune only for the fall crop. This involves cutting down the canes that would produce in July, so that the vigor of the plants all goes into the new canes that fruit in September and October. That fall crop is almost worth its weight in gold on the city market. I've seen fall red raspberries sell in New York for $1.25 a *half*-pint.

There has been a sort of decline in raspberry production for the fresh market in many areas because of diseases, especially mosaic. Virus-free plants are now available, though relatively expensive. Aphids carry virus diseases from infected plants to healthy ones. But even if you spray healthy plants for aphids, the bugs can transmit the diseases before the spray kills them. Some horticulturists are advising growers to mulch raspberries with aluminum foil, since the foil seems to scare aphids away. Don't plant your reds next to your blacks (the blacks are most susceptible to mosaic), and try not to plant any varieties close to wild raspberries or blackberries. Wild blackberries especially are full of mosaic (but they go on producing pretty well anyway).

July also begins the sweet corn trade in the North. In my book, sweet corn is the easiest of all vegetables to grow and harvest. But that simply means you have more competition from other sellers. Ditto for tomatoes. Asparagus and sweet corn are easier to sell than most vegetables, because they require the least preparation to get on the table. Housewives are well aware of this. You should be, too.

August: Think peaches and muskmelons for extra money. A quality, tree-ripened peach is hard to come by in the supermarket. They are a good seller for the smaller gardener. The advantage of a muskmelon is that it sells for about the same price as a quart of strawberries, but takes only about two seconds to pick. Buying a good muskmelon is a matter of luck. But if you raise yours correctly and pick them ripe, more of yours will be sweet and you'll have more satisfied customers than the grocery store normally has. Melons generally seem to do better on a light soil rather than a heavy one. But I get good results from my clay, which has been "lightened" over the years with plenty of organic mulch. Where you want to grow cantaloupes, lime well the year before. Then at planting time —for all melons—put a forkful of rotted manure in a hole, cover with dirt, and plant the melon seeds on top.

September: August is over and dog days gone; you suddenly feel like working again. Try to resist the temptation. The cicadas are singing and frost is on the way. And all that bounty of the garden is lying out there in the hazy sun amid the weeds that escaped your summer hoe.

What can you sell from your homestead that every other gardener is not selling? Commercial growers have the apple business pretty well in hand, and the little guy finds it hard to compete. However, if there are people in your neighborhood who really know apples, you might be able to do a little marketing of varieties like Macoun, Stayman Winesap, Grimes Golden, McIntosh, Jonathan, and other kinds that don't get into the commercial trade as much as Red and Yellow Delicious. I'm afraid that the younger generations think the Delicious are the only apples that exist. Not all progress is forward.

Dessert grapes offer an opportunity for the small gardener. A couple of vines of Concord, Niagara, and Catawba ought to be standard in all northern gardens. I won't make any friends by saying so, but ripe Concord grapes out-taste California table grapes all hollow. But as with most fruit, the best grapes to eat can't usually be shipped very far and won't last long once picked.

You cannot win your pin as a full-fledged Paradiser until you've learned how to make grape wine. And when you serve it to guests instead of highballs, grapes may suddenly become the most profitable crop you raise.

You can make your own grape juice, too. This is the only instance where I've never been able to make something that tastes as good as what we buy. But we keep trying.

I know of at least one small, part-time grape grower who has hit upon a profitable scheme that doesn't involve too much of his time. He has taken advantage of the current renewed interest in home winemaking and sells his grapes to individuals who like to make wine but not grow grapes.

October: From the pleasant work of two weekends amid the fall foliage, we sold $60 worth of bittersweet to garden stores last October. Before that, I used to spend at least one weekend hacking the miserable stuff out of my fencerows. It's amazing how quickly a noxious weed becomes a precious ornamental when it's marketable. But I wouldn't go around planting bittersweet near any other kind of ornamental. About the only plant it can't get the better of is Japanese honeysuckle. Which gives me an excuse to share a perfect example of how to live with nature rather than trying to control her.

Faced with a property line completely overgrown with multiflora rose, planted there by some misanthrope, I at first figured I would have to grub it all out to keep my two acres from becoming a jungle. While hacking at the bittersweet, I thought of another scheme. Carrying coals to Newcastle, I started planting the voracious vine among the multiflora rose. "Now, you two blasted enemies of mankind," I growled, "fight it out."

And how they have been fighting. At each other's throats from spring to fall, they have little strength left to wander out into the lawn and strangle bushes, small trees, and unwary children. I get the benefit of those "beautiful, sweet-smelling rose blossoms" in June, the red rose hips and orange bittersweet all winter long. And $60. Plus an impenetrable wall that makes my acres almost as private as a boudoir.

In the interests of science, I must admit that the two plants did not kill each other off. But they move out into the lawn only a foot a year now instead of three. I still have to hack, but not quite as much.

Lots of people sell pumpkins before Halloween. For

jack-o'-lanterns, a pumpkin is a pumpkin, but one gardener I know uses a trick to make his sell faster. When the pumpkin is small and green, he scratches names into the still-soft skin of the outer rind. As the pumpkin grows, so do the letters. It stands to reason that a boy named Joe (or his mother) will buy a pumpkin with Joe on it faster than one with nothing on it. Trouble, is, you can't get away with short names like Joe and Bob and Mary anymore. They're all Jennifers, Jeffreys, and Jessicas.

The most unique way of selling pumpkins I've heard of was "developed" by a farmer in Maryland who claimed that one year he made more money from 16 acres of pumpkins than from 3,000 acres of corn. He simply pulled a wagon full of the big yellow globes out along the road. To the wagon wheel he chained a sealed milk can with a slit in it so customers could deposit their 50¢ per pumpkin.

"Hang a big sign up, Pumpkins for Sale, and the price. Then *go away*," he says. "For some reason, more people stop and buy if I'm not standing there. Sometimes I watch from a distance. It's a circus. Women and kids climb all over in the wagon, maybe take five or six pumpkins down and line them up on the ground, trying to pick out the best one. They really seem to enjoy it. They put back the ones they don't want and put their money in the can. It's amazing. Oh, I suppose we lose a few, but most people are honest — at least in a situation like this."

Another gardener I know hit upon an idea that is sheer genius. He put up two stands, one on either side of the road, but not quite across from each other. He got his brother to run one stand, and he took charge of the other. At one stand, pumpkins sold 25¢ higher than at the other, and, of course, everyone flocked to the cheaper stand. "They thought they were getting a bargain. There were folks buying pumpkins who 15 minutes earlier didn't know they wanted one."

I've come to the conclusion that people will buy almost anything, and some wares I've seen in garden stores and gift shops in October may give you an idea:

Schemes to Make Money on the Side

1. Necklaces of buckeyes, acorns, various types of seeds. Also earrings and bracelets of same.
2. Rocks. Sometimes polished, sometimes not. Geodes, those warty stones that are hollow inside and encrusted with crystals, can be picked up in southern Indiana streams by the truckload, but cut in half, polished, and made into ashtrays, they are $40 each in a Bucks County, Pennsylvania, gift store. (Kids used to sell them at roadside in Indiana for 50¢ each years ago. I'm sure their price has gone up.) Speaking of rocks, an enterprising character in my neck of the woods sells moss-covered boulders, which he finds along the river, to suburbanites who are looking for Japanese accent pieces on their ruglike lawns. It takes a pickup truck and two very strong men.
3. Stalks of ripened wheat, natural or dyed in a variety of colors—10¢ a stalk.
4. Bunches of cattails are elegant in a vase. Also many kinds of dried weeds, reeds, and grasses for the same purpose. Giant foxtail really looks good in an umbrella stand.
5. Indian corn and that small, deep maroon strawberry popcorn. After you use the latter for Thanksgiving decorations, you can pop it. I raised and sold some one year for a nickel an ear. You have to pull the husks back tenderly and tie three ears together. Time-consuming. But at least in the East, it sells very fast.
6. Bundles of cornstalks. So help me. People like to make their own corn shocks to go with the pumpkin on the porch at Thanksgiving.
7. Wild fruit jams and jellies. Two women I've gotten to know run a roadside stand where they sell homemade jams and jellies made out of just about everything—including corncobs. A large portion of their assortment comes free for the picking from their woods and meadows: wild

197

strawberries, raspberries, wineberries, blackberries, elderberries, ground-cherries, persimmons, and crab apples. No papaws, I'm
sorry to say.

November: Tourists haven't discovered November
yet, thank God. November can give you the worst weather
of the year sometimes, but we country rovers know a secret:
A nice day in November is the nicest day of all. A warm,
lazy-hazy sky day. Bluegrass has gone into its second growth
and is green and fresh. There are no bugs. No traffic jams.
Norway maples and weeping willows are still yellow and
green. Flashes of red in the oaks seem all the more beautiful
now that the woods is mostly brown. With much of the
foliage gone you can see the bones of the countryside: the
way the hills roll, the quaint old farmsteads that have
been hidden all summer by leaves. Early November is an
Andrew Wyeth painting. Cherish it before the snow comes
blasting out of the north.

A practical thing to sell in November is cider. Almost
anywhere you are situated, you can find someone in the
area who understands the true values of life; he will own
a big cider press. You can take a load of apples over and
get them pressed out and the juice put into barrels. The
barrels will cost you a little money, but they should
last forever.

If you have egg customers dropping in on a crisp
November day, and you should happen to draw them a
glass of beady cider from one of your barrels, they will
almost certainly want to buy a gallon to take home. One
roadside-stand operator sells cider through a coin-operated
system he rigged up himself. The customer sticks two quarters in a slot above a barrel that protrudes from the wall
of his salesroom. Behind the wall is a long belt, loaded with
plastic jugs of cider. The coins trip a solenoid switch that
starts a motor and moves the belt ahead one jug's worth.
The jug slides down a little ramp, through the wall, and
into the "barrel" where the customer picks it up. Other
roadside standers fix up a fake barrel with a spigot on it.

Behind the wall is a tank of cider which flows through a plastic tube through the wall to the spigot. The customer fills his jug or glass himself. The system preserves the old, romantic cider barrel. Without the bother of the old, romantic cider barrel. P. T. Barnum said "There's a sucker born every minute," but I am equally certain there is a genius born every half hour.

December: Think Christmas and the land will give you something to sell. Bunches of holly, well fruited with berries, are a good bet if your land and climate are right for holly. Two elderly (but very young at heart) gentlemen in Maryland went into the holly business after they retired. They planted a holly orchard beforehand so that the trees were ready to bear when they were ready to retire. About the first of December they begin to trim their trees and make up nice bunches from the trimmings, which they sell wrapped in clear plastic for $1 a pound. They tell me they can clear about $1,000 by Christmas without making a big, trying, commercial job out of it.

Other families in various parts of the country make evergreen garlands and wreaths from their native greens. Here again you can make money in proportion to how hard you want to work. If you make 20 wreaths at $5 each, well, who can't use an extra $100 at Christmastime? Other people I know make up wreaths for Christmas presents. As gifts, your own handmade offerings mean more to your friends than the $10 bauble you would have purchased. You have invested your own affectionate labor in that wreath, your friends are most pleased, and you have saved a lot of money. Saving equals making.

Chapter 18

She Loves Me,
She Loves Me Not—
and Other Ways
to Enjoy Flowers

Horticulturists often draw a sharp line between flower gardening and fruit and vegetable gardening. Here is my flower garden; here is my orchard; here is my vegetable patch; here are my blasted weeds. Flowers are for heavenly poetry; vegetables are mundane prose; weeds are unspeakable blasphemies.

Pity. That kind of psychology leads only to a great deal of unnecessary work. In my little Eden, I am discovering with exquisite pleasure that every plant has a flower, and every flower is beautiful.

For proof, I just lie down in my knee-deep grass that should have been mowed, herbicided, sweated over, and cussed at least three weeks ago. Look at those flowers, all noxious weeds. I defy you to find any blooms more exotic in the most exotic of arboretums. Just see them as my children do and *look* long and deep at these marvelous little creations. And all you have to do to get them to grow is to stop running that infernal mower and sprayer every week. A child knows. If dandelions were very difficult to raise, they'd cost $4 a plant at your local greenhouse.

Ways to Enjoy Flowers

Some of the prettiest spring flowers grow on trees that are not considered "flowering" types. A sugar maple sports delicate greenish white blossoms before the leaves appear. Against a blue April sky . . . well, I'll put a cluster up against anybody's weeping cherry. Norway maples have red blossoms as sensational as orchids — if you're in the right frame of mind.

If you're mainly a vegetable gardener or orchardist, don't let anybody say you don't appreciate flowers. Take him with you under your apple trees in May. Let him consider a strawberry or squash blossom down on his hands and knees, the way you see it.

My appreciation for domesticated flowers has grown only slowly. First of all, I have almost always been hungry, and I wasn't interested in raising anything I couldn't eat. Besides, I was brought up in a country where men were big, brawny, muscle-bound types who considered flowers effeminate. Flowers were an idle but harmless pastime for the "wimmenfolks." The heroes of my childhood would rather die than admit to other males that they really enjoyed lilacs and tulips around the house.

But as time went by, I began to understand flowers. When he thought no one else would catch him, my father used to pick a bouquet of Saint Joseph's lilies and bring them into the house for Mother — a big, clumsy fistful of them along with anything else he could find blooming. Mom would kiss him and arrange the flowers very carefully on the dinner table. And when he came in at noon to eat, they would smile at each other over the flowers.

Then, not so many years ago, our preschool son and daughter marched into the house, each bringing us an armload of irises plucked unceremoniously from my wife's showplace garden. Out the window, we could see said garden, looking as if a flock of sheep had wandered through it. But there was such pride and love in those little eyes, who could care? That's what flowers are for.

Anyhow, I am beginning to like flowers as such. I especially like old-fashioned flowers that come up without any help, year after year. They take care of themselves mostly, and that is the greatest compliment you can pay a plant. They have proven themselves ecologically sound in my territory; they survive. Hollyhocks, peonies, lilacs, flags, lilies of the valley, violets, wisteria—they outlast the houses they were planted to adorn.

But more than likely I favor these flowers because of the memories attached to them. A line of flags along the brick sidewalk of my old home. A row of peonies marking a long-gone picket fence my father made. A lilac bush beside the back doorstep to the kitchen—or where the doorstep used to be. Hollyhocks rank beside the privy of yesterday and along the chicken coop that isn't there anymore; lilies of the valley on the shady north side of the house. And a gnarled old wisteria vine that snaked all the way up the windmill till its tentacles brushed against the whirling blades and made a sort of tinkling music that became more a part of me than my flesh. These are my soul flowers. They have something to do with the culture imbedded in me. They will grow, always, on my Two Acre Eden.

However, floriculture still remains, on my place, the main province of the female side of the family. She can tell you all about roses and bulbs and annuals—not me. Flowers only confuse me. For instance, when a petunia seed sprouts and begins to grow, it is more fragile than a poem not yet written down. One well-placed raindrop could assassinate it. So any petunia grower worth his potting soil starts the seeds inside, out of harm's way, and sets the plants outside after they develop a little muscle. But every year on the mound of dirt and boulders we refer to with poetic license as a rock garden, there will come up all by itself a little old-fashioned purple petunia. Just for the sake of science, I've tried planting F_1 generation, hybrid petunia seed on that spot. Dismal failure.

I leave this and other mysteries for my wife to figure out. All I know is that there is no more beautiful sight in the garden than her annuals—when she is puttering among them in her bikini.

One of the most remarkable gardeners I've ever

met is a schoolteacher whose garden has more plants and flowers per square foot than anyplace since the Hanging Gardens of ancient Babylon. When she ran out of ground in the tiny lawn around her house to grow flowers, she took to the air. Pots of plants and flowers hang in every conceivable type of planter from trees, posts, and walls. The porch is a gallery of potted plants. How many? Mary shrugs. "Last time I counted I had over 600," she says.

Mary isn't a gardener really. She's a plant doctor. The reason she has so many plants is because she cannot bear to see one die. "Everybody brings me sick or unwanted plants, and I can't bring myself to throw them away. It is so much fun to make them healthy again, and by that time they are members of the family."

All her 600 potted plants and uncounted hundreds of other flowers around the house are so placed to get the right amount of sunshine they need, no more and no less. I saw only one plant out of place, a very small and delicate Japanese maple tree. "That's there on purpose," she explained. "That tree is about 15 years old. It doesn't get enough light to grow properly. Challenging—just to keep it alive. It's sort of a natural bonsai."

Mary can tend all her potted plants in a half hour— "if I don't stop to talk to them." She simply walks around with a hose and gives each a drink. "The most difficult part of growing potted plants is knowing just how much water to give them," she says. "It's so easy to overwater."

Mary makes her own potting soil. She mixes compost from her heap with sand, garden loam, and sometimes a little peat. "You have to vary the mixture according to what plant you're growing. You just have to learn that," she says. Her favorite fertilizer is fish emulsion.

The variety of her plants is exceeded only by the kinds of ingenious planters she grows them in. Clay and ceramic pots, iron kettles, wire baskets, almost anything that will hold dirt, including rocks with naturally hollowed-out pockets in them. Wherever she goes, Mary keeps a sharp eye for cheap, unique containers. She showed me some blocks of wood, deeply dished on one side, discarded by a factory that makes wooden bowls. "They throw these blocks away after their machines cut as many bowls as possible out of them. They'll make beautiful planters after I sand them a little."

Her latest project is to combine driftwood and potted flowers into pleasing artistic arrangements. Walking in the woods or along a river, her sharp eyes will spot an unusually striking piece of gnarled tree root or twisted weather-worn limb. She takes it home and cleans out the rotted wood and dirt, if any, with wire brushes. Depending on its shape, she'll use it in conjunction with an already potted plant, or make a pot in a hollow of the wood, from which a plant or flower can grow.

Her creations gripped the imagination of my family. For several months after our visit with Mary, we returned from every woodland walk laden with "driftwood." The kids got the hang of it almost immediately. They saw beauty in every dead stick that lay in their paths. By the time we had walked 100 yards, each had an armload. As a result, we have about half a cord of dead wood in the garage, some of which will never be combined with anything except the flames of the winter fireplace. But a couple of our "driftwood-potted plants" don't look bad at all, and we have visions of selling our masterpieces at exorbitant prices "someday."

There are housewives all over the country who turn their knowledge of flowers into a little spending money every year. I know two farmwives who team up and plant about an acre of mums every year and sell them right out of the field. They lift the "mother" mums in the fall, put them in cold frames for the winter, then transfer them in February to a small greenhouse, where the plants start to grow. The new shoots are clipped and rooted in a sterile growing medium. About the last week in May, the two women set the plants out in the field. By the last of September, the mums are blooming beautifully. Customers come and dig their own plants to take home and put in their flower beds. The two gals pocketed about $2,000 last fall.

I stopped at a roadside stand one day, curious about

a large planting of gladiolus in the field next to the market. "I sell them as cut flowers," the owner explained. "People who stop by for a melon or a dozen ears of corn can't resist taking a bouquet home. I can grow glads in rows, like corn, and cultivate them with the tractor." How does he dig up all those bulbs? "Use the potato digger. Works fine."

Another neighbor woman (if you get the idea that all our neighbors are avid gardeners, you are just about correct) makes a hobby of breeding irises in an effort to reach two specific goals, either of which could be money in the bank. The big bearded irises are not only beautiful but are fairly simple to hybridize. But no one has yet bred a truly red iris. So neighbor Isabel is trying to create one by crossing strains that shade from orange pink to reddish brown. If she ever succeeds in realizing her goal, the red bloom could be worth a small fortune. The fact that professional hybridizers keep attempting this feat all over the world without success doesn't deter her in the least. "It'll be someone just like me who doesn't know all the facts that'll do it," she says. And I think she's right.

Her other iris project is to grow a crop that blooms again in the fall. Irises that will bloom twice a year aren't so common, and those that do often cannot boast the quality of the best spring-blooming hybrids. Before she and her husband moved away, Isabel had two bulbs that bloomed again in the fall, and they were multiplying only very slowly. She allowed us to take "any iris you want EXCEPT the fall bloomers and that reddish one down there at the end of the row." These she took with her.

My wife thinks irises are the most satisfying flower to grow, as long as she can get me to dig up the rhizomes and help replant them in August. "Good irises are as pretty as orchids to me," she says. "And so much easier to grow."

About the only fault we find with them is the blasted iris borer, which, if left unhampered, will enter a plant through one of the big bladed leaves and tunnel on down to the rhizome and eat it completely. My wife watches the plants closely in early summer, and when she spots a tunnel beginning (you can tell by the little pile of chewed leaf

205

the worm leaves at the entrance), she pounces on the borer with very unfeminine malice. Carol says if you don't dig up the plants every other year and throw away old and diseased roots, you can expect trouble. At least that's what she tells me so I will dig them up. Iris is one plant that doesn't take mulching very well. The mulch may rot the rhizomes if piled too closely to them.

Strawflowers have become a family favorite of ours, again because of our never-ending quest for low-labor money-making possibilities. Our interest in them began with a visit to one of those numerous little roadside knick-knack shops with which the East is blessed. Hanging all over one wall of this particular shop were bunches of bright flowers. "They're artificial," I stated unctuously. "They can't be," retorted my wife. "They're too nice."

"They're strawflowers," said the shop owner. "You just dry them and they'll last all winter. Only a dollar a bunch."

I looked at Carol and she looked at me. The dollar signs in my eyes were reflected in hers. Both of us saw immediately 40 acres of strawflowers sown with a tractor and grain drill, then cut and bundled by a miniature grain binder which we would of course invent ourselves.

"There would probably be 150,000 bunches to the acre," I mumbled. Carol giggled. The shop owner stared. Shop owners are used to nuts.

The next year we planted strawflowers. A whole 1/320th of an acre. We had "fresh" flowers in our vases all winter. And just as soon as we find time. . . .

It is interesting to me to note how many people think of growing flowers for pleasure and how few think of them as sideline profit too. A couple of years ago, a farmer in Florida nearly became a millionaire by practically cornering the market for baby's breath. He grows the major portion of the whole national crop. Another farmer capitalized on crown vetch, a cover plant for problem areas that recently became quite popular with home owners because of its colorful blooms. He told me he sold $1,000 worth of crown vetch roots off an area "not much bigger than a good-sized living room."

As the standard of living increases in this country (at least everyone says it's increasing—costs are, anyway), I'm sure the market is going to grow for flowers. I think housewives who like to garden are missing an opportunity. For instance, Carol took a peck of Regal lily bulbs down to the garden center store where we deal and sold them. Just like that.

The store owner knows us, of course—we're always trying to sell him surplus from our gardens—and realizes we won't try to palm off any diseased plants. But any conscientious gardener can establish the same kind of relationship with market outlets in his area.

Friends of ours have contracted to supply several garden stores with flats of euonymous and pachysandra, 50 rooted cuttings per flat. They have 200 flats sitting in a shady edge of their lawn, nearly ready for delivery. The cuttings came from their own plantings, which they grew on the part of their lawn that was too steep to mow.

Garden-store suppliers and landscapers are often more than willing to farm out the growing of some kinds of plants—especially where a lot of handwork and attention to detail are involved. With labor at a premium, it's often cheaper that way.

Interest in flowers has turned us into thieves. We don't go around digging up wild flowers. Some people do that—and the flowers often die before the erstwhile thief gets them planted again properly—which is an abomination and against the law in many instances. But we swipe seeds. We wander through public parks noting every odd flowering bush or tree. Later, when said plants have gone to seed, we wander again, furtively stuffing seeds in our pockets, which is worse than nutty. I'm sure no one really cares. We do the same thing along city streets.

Lately we have been pocketing every acorn we chance upon. Unfortunately, we read about one of those "old practices" in a mildewed book we dredged off a back shelf of a used-book store. We can never resist "old practices." It seems that people used to save a few choice, fat acorns until December, then put them in planters, three to a pot, with moist sphagnum moss. The acorns sprout, says the book, into beautiful little oak seedlings just as pretty, in some people's view, as a pot of poinsettias or a bunch of holly. We will of course try it this December. After which I will probably be able to impart some tremendously vital information, like: Acorns grow better squirrels than they do poinsettias.

Everybody ought to have some roses, and I know a cheap way to get them if you aren't in a hurry. You don't collect seeds; you snip off cuttings. This requires the knowledge and approval of the owner. So you have friends who have roses. Everybody has a friend who has roses. You make it a point to drop by in early spring when he is out trimming his bushes. He is only too glad to let you snip off some nice green cuttings about six inches long. You take them home and shove them into the newly thawed ground, leaving about an inch above ground. Then you put a glass mason jar over the cutting. Then you go away and pray. About half the time, the cutting will root, and by and by, you can lift the jar off and your rose bush will slowly begin to grow. This is not a particularly practical way to grow roses, but it's cheap. My grandmother got a whole garden full that way.

Chapter 19

How to Beat Winter

Among my pines, hope is always green. Winter and its harsh, despairing reminder of ultimate death never really penetrates there. So that is where I stand on this gray white, dismal January afternoon. I avoid looking at the snow; I concentrate on pine needles and the bittersweet berries on the fence beyond. In a patch of brown grass, an overwintering robin alights, a stubborn fellow who decided Florida was not for him either. He looks for a windblown weed seed, finds none. Eyes the bittersweet. He is hungry enough now to eat even those acid berries. He pecks into one, shakes his head, looks at me. We share the brightness of the orange berry, we understand the bitterness of the taste, and of the wind. We share the vigil in the pines, relishing bittersweet. We wait for springtime.

In less poetic terms, I loathe cold weather and a land barren of green growing things. I dedicate the poetry to all gardeners, who on January 2, suffering not from possible frostbite but holiday hangover, begin to yearn for lilacs and freshly plowed soil. Three more months yet to wait.

The words stick in my throat—you have to learn to enjoy winter. To the country gardener, that's downright cloying. Enjoy four-foot drifts to the barn? Laugh as the car skids into a lonely ditch? Frolic in goppy mud up to your knees? Bask in the bone-chilling wind roaring across that patch of land that somewhere dim in memory was once a garden?

But winter can be beautiful. All it takes is an appreciative eye and thermal underwear. A daily walk over your country acres in winter will reveal almost as much color, though in much more subdued tones, as a summer walk. Green remains alive in mosses and evergreens; red in the flash of a pheasant neck, in ice-covered rose hips along the hedge, in haw apples, holly berries and half a score of wild woodland bush fruits whose names I don't know. In winter one depends on the sky itself for blue, and the snow will reflect that blue in a dozen muted shades. Against the snow, rocks and trees and dead rattling weeds shade to magnificent grays and blacks in contrast. Yellows remain in ground-cherries surviving just above the snow; in ears of corn left by the harvester, in the very cornstalks themselves —and the low winter sun slants its rays almost sideways at these objects, picking out a grainy gold one never sees in summer. And the browns. Leaf brown, tree trunk brown, barn siding brown, cattail brown, dead grass brown.

Nature is never dead. Hardly has the last maple leaf fallen, when, with the first January thaw, the buds begin to swell again. Even into late November, the witch hazel is blooming in the woods, and in February, the snowdrops push up through icy ground, ignoring blizzards. Even as far north as the Ohio River valley, the mistletoe berries still hang pearly and glistening in January's sun. And in coldest Minnesota I have gathered fresh watercress from spring-fed streams when the temperature was below zero.

Nor does your more domesticated garden need to be completely dormant through the winter. Last year on New Year's Day we gathered most of our dinner directly from the land (Zone IV), despite the fact that a foot of snow covered the ground.

How to Beat Winter

At the onset of cold weather, I had covered the row of winter greens (planted in early July) with clear plastic roofing sheets. Pushing aside the snow and lifting the protective covering, I picked a dishpanful of excellent endive and kale, and the last two leeks. From under a mound of leaves, I dug up potatoes and carrots unscathed by cold weather or frozen ground.

We drank beady cider from our very last apples, each cupful warmed and with a stick of cinnamon poked into it. Our dessert was hickory nut pie — the nuts foraged in November. The roasted pheasant came from the freezer and before that from the cornfield.

There are other tricks of winter gardening. Clumps of rhubarb roots, witloof chicory, and even asparagus can be dug and stored in the fall, then "forced" in the cellar for winter eating. Rhubarb is the easiest to force, and actually produces a better-tasting stalk in the cool darkness of the cellar than it does out in the garden in spring.

The principle behind forcing is that by fall the plant roots have stored up enough nourishment to produce a crop without further supplies of food energy. All you do is plant the roots in almost any kind of growing medium and water them. But once forced, a root is finished for good.

Before the advent of high-speed transportation and frozen foods, the art of forcing many kinds of plants for winter use was common practice. By using cold frames and hotbeds extensively — not to mention greenhouses — commercial gardeners could provide fresh vegetables all winter, for those who could afford to buy them.

Of course, the best way to beat winter is with a greenhouse. With the advent of plastic, there are so many styles of greenhouses at so many different prices, I hesitate to talk about the subject. Glass is more expensive than plastics and fiberglasses. It is my belief that one is better off with glass if he can afford it; that he is better off with a more expensive plastic than a cheaper one. (Not only will it last longer, but because it is structurally stronger, it requires less underbracing than the cheaper grades, thus lowering the cost of the entire building.) I have been in many greenhouses, and I no longer advise the small gardener to build a greenhouse of plastic *film*. Stick to the semirigid panels. They last longer and look better.

Another of my harebrained ideas, which I intend to try when I get rich, is to combine a greenhouse with that other great winter beater, an indoor swimming pool for a heat sink. A pool down the center of a greenhouse? Why not? There must be someone who has done this.

So much information about greenhouses is turned out, there is no need for me to say more. Garden stores and greenhouse manufacturers have dispersed enough literature to stuff a library. Read it all and then spend some time looking at greenhouses and talking to greenhouse operators before buying.

A friend of mine built a greenhouse on the east side of his house, over a cellar window. The opened window provides enough heat to keep the small house warm. He framed the building (actually a lean-to) with two by fours and covered it with corrugated plastic panels. Out-of-pocket money spent was under $50, he says.

For several years, I've been raising plants in what was once a breezeway between the house and the garage. I. walled off both ends, and roofed the room with fiberglass panels. The translucency of both my fiberglass and my friend's plastic panels seem to be suitable for both sun- and shade-loving plants, and some plastic companies have assured me this is true.

Most greenhouse-less gardeners can content themselves through the winter with houseplants. But a few intrepid souls decide to pretend snow doesn't exist and go right on flower gardening outdoors. M. M. Graff, in an intriguing book *Flowers in the Winter Garden* (Garden City, New York: Doubleday, 1966), tells about her winter gardens (in New Jersey and on Long Island) where she has induced alpine plants like crocuses and snowdrops to bloom even in January. The trick, among others, is to make full use of the concept of microclimate.

For instance, on a cold, sunny day in January, the temperature out in the open may be 10 degrees, but on the ground along a south-facing wall, it may shoot up to 70. A plant living in that restricted area will bloom faster than one out in the open. Likewise a strong airflow on a hillside can keep a plant from freezing though the temperature is the same as in a still, low pocket where the plant *does* freeze. That is one reason why you will find very productive apple and peach orchards on steep mountainsides where the weather gets cold enough to freeze a brass monkey.

But with or without the skill or knowledge of making alpine flowers bloom in a January snowstorm, you can preserve the feeling of summer around your place all winter. Grow as many evergreen trees — pine, spruce, hemlock, yew — as you can. Evergreens may not always seem the best trees for shade, but they are, as a group, certainly the cleanest lawn trees. Evergreens make excellent windbreaks and provide more privacy. Living among them, winter never seems too harsh.

Also, broad-leaved evergreen bushes like azaleas and rhododendrons remain green all winter, where they are hardy, and soften barren January.

Some ferns and most mosses will remain green well into January, if not all winter. If you have a winter garden with a big rock in it, get moss to grow on the rock, and a few ferns on the north side of it.

We have a protected spot under some yews that is much too shady for grass. Here we plant ferns among which we place pieces of logs or rotten tree branches that are covered with moss, which we find in the woods. Whenever we spot a new kind of moss (new to us), we bring a clump home and try to get it established in our moss garden. It keeps growing until after Christmas.

Our little white Christmas rose blooms nearly until the holidays. The bittersweet, of course, lasts until February. As do fire thorn berries. Pachysandra flourishes about as well, it seems, in early winter as in summer. Along about February 10, even a green sprig of Japanese honeysuckle (which I am sure could grow with equal ease in hell or Antarctica) looks pretty good.

Two Acre Eden

Winter-fighting gardeners ought to know about the uncommon habits of witch hazel. Common witch hazel (hardy to Zone III) blooms in the woods in November. Japanese and Chinese witch hazel (hardy to Zone V) bloom lemon yellow in February and March.

Norway maples hold their leaves well into November (some individual specimens more so than others), a fact that can be used to stretch fall two weeks longer in the North. One year in central New York State, I passed a farmstead that looked magnificently summery on November 10, simply because it stood amid some 20 huge Norway maples that were still green and fully leaved. The farm looked like an oasis in the brown countryside.

The weeping willow is another common tree that can shorten winter a little. It holds its green leaves into November, too. It has the added advantage of being about the first of the large trees to leaf out in the spring. Even before the leaves open, the branches begin to turn greenish yellow with the first, warm March days.

Perhaps such observations are not as important to some people as to others. Having lived very close to nature through some long and barren winters, I value green foliage as a great psychological help in overcoming the malaise and moroseness of the bitter winter moons. A Minnesota farmer knows what I mean.

Chapter 20

Bored?
You Have to Be Kidding

Returning to the land is almost always the idea of the male. Women, who are much the saner sex, resist the notion as long as possible. Sometimes they are able to stall until the temptation passes, thereby saving many unfit husbands from coming to grief and failure as modern homesteaders. Women understand instinctively what the game is all about; while the male dreams of independence and the simple life, the female knows that under any circumstances she'll still have washing to do, will freeze or can a truckload of vegetables, and keep the home fires burning—literally.

Oddly enough though, once the man can be put off no longer and decides, come hell or high water, that he *will* sojourn in the countryside, it is the wife who steps in with practicality and makes the idea work, if it is at all workable. While husband rushes frantically about the new homestead asserting his territorial imperative in his spare hours away from his outside job, she plods along finishing the projects he starts: feeding the chickens he bought, weeding the corn he planted, sanding the furniture he nailed together, painting the barn he almost built, mowing the grass he overfertilized. When the cow is calving, when the sheep break through the fence, when the roof begins to leak, when the well pump breaks down, the husband is off someplace trying to make enough money to buy a secondhand pickup truck, which she will have to learn to enjoy driving, not to mention learn how to enjoy changing tires on.

Why do they do it? I don't know.

"Why do you do it?" I asked my wife along about 11:00 P.M. as she was just finishing cleaning and freezing three chickens while I was finishing watching the Monday night movie on TV.

"Why do I do what?"

"Why do you go along with this madness of raising our own food and pretending like we are homesteading a virgin wilderness."

"A what kind of wilderness?"

"Cut it out. Why do you go out there and dig potatoes and cut bittersweet and pick strawberries and freeze 87 pints of corn when you could be out helping the PTA or earning a good wage someplace."

"Now wait a minute. It was your idea not mine. You're the one who plowed up the whole backyard and built that barn that Daddy says is going to fall down and hurt someone."

"I'm sorry I asked. Just skip it."

"Well, look. The only thing the men we know really want is to get out of the rat race. And then I listen to a bunch of women talking, and all they want to do is get into the rat race. They have the nicest homes in the country, and all they can think about is getting liberated by going to work someplace. Can you imagine that? Getting liberated by going to work someplace. Can you imagine that? Getting liberated by going to work for someone else. Good grief. And then I talk to women who *have* to work someplace, and they all complain they don't get enough time off. Everybody's nuts!"

"That doesn't explain you. . . ."

"Well, I don't care what people say about me." She hesitated, and I could tell by the look on her face, that she had thought of something brilliant, at least in her estimation.

"*That's* why I do it," she exclaimed suddenly.

"What's that?"

"I just told you. I don't care what people might think about my opinions. I don't *have* to care. I'm as free as you can get in America. No bosses to please, no public to appease, no image to uphold, no position to strive for, no votes to get. The housewife has gained the independence everyone is seeking. I have to answer only to you, and you don't care what I say. I've got one boss—how's that for women's lib?"

"Can I trade in the car for a pickup truck?"

"No."

"But you just said a little bit ago that I was—"

"I know what I said. The answer is still no."

Deciding there was no future in interviewing one's wife, I shook the dust of home from my shoes and went to visit what is perhaps the best example of everything I've tried to say in this book. This couple—I guess I'll just call them Joe and Alice at the risk of sounding like a second-rate, X-rated movie—and their four children, 17, 14, 9, and 6, live on a 120-acre farm. Joe has a good job in town, about a ten-minute drive from home. The farm makes a small profit outright, but in addition, it provides a rich abundance of good food, hobbies, recreation, and a sense of worth and wonder.

Joe is buying the farm, dollar by agonizing dollar. At first he tried full-time farming, but an unfortunate accident to his herd of cows together with dwindling chances for making a profitable living on a small farm forced him to seek off-farm employment to supplement his income.

Alice was a city girl who has taken to country life. She enjoys hunting; fishing; gardening; collecting antiques; working with livestock; cooking; coaching the girl's softball, volleyball, and basketball teams at school (and playing same); bird-watching; square dancing; hiking; hunting arrowheads in the fields and wild berries in the fence lines;

entertaining; camping; and above all, providing her family by the sweat of her brow with almost all the food they eat.

It seemed like a ridiculous question, but I asked her anyhow: "Don't you feel bored and unfulfilled slaving away out here in the country, you—you—you housewife, you?"

A silvery gale of tinkling, joyous female laughter. "Bored? You've got to be kidding," she replied. "Boredom is a disease of the mind. It has nothing to do with your environment. A woman who is bored in her home will be bored anyplace on earth. It's like happiness. You have to learn to enjoy what you have at any given time in your life, even during hard times. Then if things get better, you can enjoy life more. People who don't learn to be happy when they have little, never learn to be happy no matter how much they get."

When it comes to living off the land and providing meal after meal without benefit of supermarkets and food processors, Alice must be the national champion. Of course it's a family enterprise. Joe does the heavier work, and the children all have their specific jobs—"That's part of the reason we do it, maybe the main part," says Joe. "Our kids are growing up with a feeling that they are really *needed.* I think one of the big reasons we seem to be having so much trouble with youth today is that our society has taken away this sense of need from the teenager. Until young people are out of college, they don't really take their proper place in society. Yet we want them to be mature and responsible. When I was a kid, Dad made me feel that he couldn't run the farm without my help. And that was a good feeling."

Joe raises corn, small grains, and hay to feed a few cattle, hogs, and chickens. The surplus grain is sold. At any given time, there are perhaps ten head of beef cattle in the barn, a couple of milk cows, a few hogs. Certain animals are special 4-H projects of the youngsters, which they raise with extra care for the fair, a possible blue ribbon, and 4-H sale. "A certain amount of money from their projects they keep and put in the bank," explains Joe. "Actually, I pay for raising the livestock, or the farm does, but they have to work for it too. It's better than just giving them money for a college education."

Enough pork and beef is kept to supply the family's needs. Alice raises special broad-breasted chickens that dress out to eight- to ten-pound roasters in five or six months. Some of the dressed poultry Joe cures and smokes along with hams and bacon. Alice has all her own eggs and milk—even makes her own butter. She also raises a few turkeys each year. Domestic meat is supplemented by wild game: deer, pheasants, rabbits, fish, sometimes even bear.

The compartments of two big freezers not stuffed with meat are crammed with fruits and vegetables. An ancient springhouse, dug deep into the ground in the back-yard over a century ago, still provides adequate storage for apples, milk, a crock of butter, and some fresh vegetables. In another corner of the yard stands a smokehouse, which Joe uses regularly. Smoked meat is hung from the rafters in the attic. There's a root cellar under the lawn too, with an entrance through the main cellar. There Alice can store potatoes or canned food if she runs out of storage space elsewhere, which often happens.

You would think that with all these avenues of processing and storing food for home use, this perky housewife would be satisfied. But not Alice. Her real hang-up is drying foods—especially corn and snap beans.

In an antique shop, she found one of those old-fashioned food dryers—a large but shallow tin pan the bottom two inches of which is an enclosed tank. You simply fill the tank with water, set the pan on the stove, and fill the upper open section with whatever you want to dry. Turn the stove down low, and the hot water slowly dries the food overnight.

I watched her doing a batch of green beans. The pods shriveled up and turned almost black and looked very unappealing. You simply store them in lidded (but not sealed) jars. A bushel of fresh beans fills only four one-quart jars when dried. My wife took a jar of them home. Surprisingly enough, once soaked and cooked, the beans looked about like canned ones but tasted much better.

Alice dries peaches and apples this way too. "I have to hide the apple schnitz," she says. "The kids all like them better than candy."

Alice makes jams and jellies and preserves and pumpkin custard for pies. She makes apple butter in a copper kettle in the oven, and knows the kind of food lore that separates the women from the girls. "Baldwin apples make the best apple butter," she says. First she cooks two quarts of cider (she makes a lot of that too) with five pounds of sugar, a teaspoon of allspice, and a sassafras twig. This concoction is mixed with applesauce and another quart of cider (enough sauce to make 13 pints of apple butter). The cooking process takes about eight hours altogether. "But the real secret is to take the sassafras twig *out* after the first four hours," Alice says.

In addition to churning butter (with the blender), the family makes homemade ice cream. But Alice's real forte is baking. She bakes bread four times a week, not to mention a steady supply of cakes and cookies.

"Four times a week?" I asked in awe.

"Yes, we have homemade bread and butter most of the time. Baking bread is my tranquilizer. Or at least kneading dough is. I know it says that in all the women's magazines now and sounds corny. But it works. I take out my frustrations on the bread dough."

"Why do you go to all the trouble of getting food on the table the hard way?" I asked.

"Well, I sort of get a kick out of it. In a way. You know food preparation really is an art, or a craft anyway. There's more to it than just work. And you can save some money, you know. Especially with the way this tribe eats. We must save $100 a month or something like that. And there's the health angle too. And all the talk about food additives and nutritionless food. We *know* what we eat. And it tastes much better."

With all this work, you'd guess that Joe and Alice have time for nothing else. Quite the opposite. They take a long vacation every year. Both are involved closely with school and community affairs. And down at the end of the long lane that skirts the farm's acres is a little grove of trees which Alice calls the Bird Sanctuary.

Actually it's her sanctuary, or Joe's or the kids', either each one in solitude or often together on a Sunday afternoon picnic. "Sometimes, I just come back here and sit and meditate for awhile," says Alice. "By the time I get back to the house, I'm ready to go again."

I've come to know a great many people who have chosen to live out in the country much like Alice and Joe and have made a success of it. I've arrived at a number of characteristics they all share, which you might very well use in judging whether or not you fit the mold.

1. First of all, to make things difficult, these people don't fit any mold, or more specifically, any of the images we have thought up for Americans. They somehow escape common labels like liberal or conservative, Silent Majority, elite snob, hard hat, egghead. None of these applies. If peole who deliberately move to the country for a less harried life can be branded philosophically at all, I'd call them moderate individualists. They don't like to be connected with any particular group except occasionally with other individuals on a personal level.

2. Indeed, if there is one characteristic common to successful sojourners in the country, it is that they begin to lose interest in anything that becomes popular. In fact, if moving to the country becomes too popular, the genuine countryman would probably consider selling his place and moving into the city. But back-to-the-landers know this will never happen. The whole trend of history is toward grouping together in cities, and that won't change. The vast majority of people fear even a few hours of solitude.

3. This characteristic really should be number one. Husbands and wives who live in the partial solitude of country life *always* like each other. They enjoy each other's company. I don't know of a single one of these couples who do not view each other as equals of a sort, profoundly respectful of each other's abilities, each expecting the other to be able to do anything he or she can do. And usually can. And between them is an open but subtle sexuality.

You can sense it but never see it. You have the feeling that ten seconds after you've driven out of the driveway, they are in passionate embrace.

4. The countryman enjoys most of all simple, sensuous experience, in moderation and without shame. In moderation because his way of life, freely chosen, demands physical discipline; without shame, because he has successfully shed the puritanism of his heritage. The true countryman is one of the few people who will admit (but only privately) that the most important things in life are good food after hunger, good drink after thirst, good sex after longing. A warm fire at the end of a cold day outdoors. A swim after blackberry picking. A pure gold sunset. The sound of water tumbling over rocks. His children laughing. Hardened muscles responding to the challenge of hard physical labor — and getting bone-tired is worth it because resting again is so delightful. The skill of disciplined fingers artfully employed. A good joke well told. The countryman understands deep down that this is what it's all about. He learns the wisdom to be content with it.

5. The countryman's view is microcosmic — like an artist's. He tends to limit himself to a fairly small world with definite boundaries and to study that world in great depth, rather than spread his knowledge thin over greater worlds. He is adept at seeing how world problems relate to his own locale and is apt to judge the seriousness of such a problem only to the extent of its applicability to his locality. He is even more adept at relating a local problem to the world at large. He knows his own place is a microcosm of the whole world; understanding his place leads him to a better understanding of all places.

A perfect example might be a wife of a young farmer I met quite by accident not long ago. When I stopped by the farm to see their dairy herd, she was raking leaves off a lawn easily more than an acre in size. Raking that many leaves surely tops most people's list of most unwanted jobs. Yet it was very apparent that she was actually enjoying the work — even making a game out of it to the delight of her two toddling children.

Later in the evening, we all gathered in the kitchen — one of those lovely, huge, old farm kitchens that remain forever the center of country life — and talked. This young couple worked long hours on their farm, George in the barn and Ann in the house. But Ann even found time for a little sideline business — clipping poodles, an art she taught herself.

But the fact that she was a most unusual woman only gradually revealed itself as the evening wore on. When I asked what problems she considered most threatening today, her answer was immediate: "Pollution, overpopulation, and education."

A predictable answer perhaps, but her reasons weren't. When she talked about pollution, she talked about the creek behind her house; about population explosion as it related to her township; about education in her school district. Unlike most young people who discuss these problems in cliches and vacuous generalities, she understood both the pros and cons and could sympathize with both sides from her own experience in specific real-life situations. And she was wise enough to admit, when the subject got beyond her own experience, that she wasn't qualified to give an opinion.

She made a point of telling me that she had not attended college, testing me, I later realized, seeing if I would categorize her in the slot that "educated" people often automatically put the High School Graduate. I suppose in a way I did, because as the conversation edged into education and religion, she reduced me to openmouthed astonishment.

She began quoting Reinhold Niebuhr and Teilhard de Chardin in the same offhand manner she used in discussing her garden. Well, it was no great thing to her. Studying philosophy and religion just happened to be one of her hobbies. She didn't agree with Spinoza, but she didn't go along with Kant either, and Buber was interesting but . . .

For an hour that kitchen became a graduate seminar in the history of philosophy, and it might have lasted longer if either her husband or I had not exhausted our knowledge of the subject.

"But you don't necessarily want your children to go to college?" I asked again.

She smiled seeing the apparent irony in her attitude.

"Well, why should they? All you have to do is get the books and read them. I just think schools have a way of limiting, not broadening, a person. I just distrust *systems*."

All the while, I had been staring at two huge freezers that dominated the kitchen.

"You must raise most of your own food," I suggested.

"Oh yes, almost all of it. A lot of work."

"Why do you do it?"

Again, that impish grin. "It's the only way I know really to beat the Establishment."

Books I Like

The publications I've listed here are so few that I can't really call this a bibliography. Nor are they necessarily the best works on subjects for Two Acre Edenites. "Best" books on gardening are generally a matter of opinion. I chose these mainly because they are my favorites and because some of them are least likely to be included in the bibliographies of hundreds of other garden books.

Several of these books are so old you can probably find them only the way I did — by haunting used-book stores. There's enough fun in that alone to justify listing them. But even though some of the information is outdated (changes in chemicals, machinery, the economic situation, and plant varieties make any garden book that is three years old "outdated"), these old books have a certain classic quality about them that reflects the spirit of the true gardener better than some modern works. And they are full of facts that can help you judge the real worth of what is "new" in gardening.

Brown, James, and Bush, Louise. *America's Garden Book.* New York: Charles Scribner's Sons, 1958.

Rockwell, F. F., ed. *Ten Thousand Garden Questions Answered by Twenty Experts.* Garden City, New York: Doubleday, 1959.

Taylor, Norman, ed. *Taylor's Encyclopedia of Gardening.* Boston: Houghton Mifflin, 1961.

These three books are not the only good general gardening works, but they are the ones I find myself most often referring to. No matter how offbeat the subject, I've always found some information on almost any phase of gardening in at least one of them.

Clark, Harold J. *Small Fruits for Your Home Garden.* Garden City, New York: Doubleday, 1958.

Kraft, Ken and Pat. *The Home Garden Cookbook: From Seed to Plate.* Garden City, New York: Doubleday, 1970.

These two books are very helpful for the gardener interested in growing his own fruits and vegetables. The second combines the "how to" of growing with recipes. A perfect addition to any Two Acre Edenite's library.

Fowles, John. "Weeds, Bugs, American." *Sports Illustrated,* 21 December, 1970, pp. 84-88.

The noted English novelist has written what I fervently wish could be a chapter in *Two Acre Eden.* So closely does he hew to the philosophy I've tried to express, one might suspect that the two of us were in cahoots. If you read nothing else in the bibliography, do look at this piece.

Johns, Glenn F., compiler; Rodale, Robert, ed. *The Basic Book of Organic Gardening.* New York: Organic Gardening®/Ballantine, 1971.

The serious organic gardener will find this book crammed with the kind of information he's looking for.

Free, Montague. *Plant Pruning in Pictures: How, When, and Where to Prune, and with What Tools.* Garden City, New York: Doubleday, 1961.

Sooner or later, every gardener has to prune, and then he finds that mere words, no matter how lucid, fail him. This book is the best I have found to tell you how to prune, with many and detailed pictures.

The Whole Earth Catalog, a publication of Portola Institute, 558 Santa Cruz, Menlo Park, CA 94025.

Modern homesteaders and country do-it-yourselfers, looking for offbeat information on subsistence living and cheaper alternatives, made this periodical a best-seller in 1970. Packed with information, but I recommend it because it's also highly entertaining reading. Unfortunately, its publication has been discontinued.

Scarseth, George D. *Man and His Earth.* Ames, Iowa: Iowa State University Press, 1962.

Scarseth, now deceased, was a soil scientist, revered by the agricultural world. I recommend his book not only as a way to understand soil better, but also to understand modern agriculture better. The urban gardener today too often is under the impression that commercial farmers and the scientists who work with them are all out for the almighty dollar at the expense of the land and the environment. Fortunately, that is far from the truth. Men like Scarseth spend their lifetimes trying to find ways to keep the world from starving to death while doing their utmost to pass on to the next generation a land richer than they found it. Such men have had a great deal more success in both of these endeavors than their shouting, but do-nothing, ecological detractors. The dilemma is not as easily solved as the backyard gardening expert sometimes believes.

Farmers' Bulletin, on sale by the Superintendent of Documents, U.S. Government Printing Office, North Cap Street NW, Washington, DC 20402.

All Two Acre Edenites should be aware of these bulletins. They cover just about every agricultural and horticultural subject you can dream up and cost little, most are only 10¢. The best way to find out about them is to call or visit the agricultural extension office in your county. The county agent there has many of the bulletins on file and can give you the numbers of any specific ones you want to send for. Don't be afraid to bother him; that's part of his job. And, by the way, he is more apt to know the answer to your gardening problems than anyone else around.

Kains, M. G. *Five Acres and Independence.* New York: Greenberg, 1935.

Pearson, Haydn. *Fifteen Ways to Make Money in the Country.* New York: Grosset and Dunlap, 1949.

———. *Success on the Small Farm.* New York: McGraw-Hill, second printing, 1946.

Terry, T. B. *Our Farming: How We Have Made a Run-Down Farm Bring Both Profit and Pleasure.* Philadelphia: The Farmer Company, 1893.

Waring, P. Allston, and Teller, Walter Magnes. *Roots in the Earth.* New York: Harper and Brothers, 1943.

These five books are all outdated, but that's what makes them valuable and fun to read. Besides, most of the information is as solid now as it was then. Only the numbers have changed. I have no idea if any of them are still in print. They are the ones I consider the most informative out of the dozens of old books I have scrounged in second-hand bookstores.

Coon, Nelson. *Using Plants for Healing.* Emmaus, Pa.: Rodale Press, 1979.

A good book for the countryman who wants to know more about the wild plants around him and how to enjoy them. Of equal value is the excellent bibliography Coon adds of other books on this popular subject.

Nell P. Nichols, ed. *The Farm Journal Freezing and Canning Cookbook: Prized Recipes from the Farms of America.* Garden City, New York: Doubleday, 1963.

A good guide to preserving the garden abundance for the cold days of winter.

Wagner, Willis. *Modern Carpentry.* South Holland, Illinois: Goodheart-Wilcox, 1969.

When you have to fix something around the house, or want to build something new (and who doesn't?), here's a book to bring you up-to-date on tools, materials, and methods.

Index

Index